RETROCULTURE

RETROCULTURE

William S. Lind

★ ★ ★ TAKING AMERICA BACK

ARKTOS
LONDON 2019

Copyright © 2019 by Arktos Media Ltd.

All rights reserved. No part of this book may be reproduced or utilised in any form or by any means (whether electronic or mechanical), including photocopying, recording or by any information storage and retrieval system, without permission in writing from the publisher.

ISBN	978-1-912975-30-3 (Paperback)
	978-1-912975-31-0 (Ebook)
EDITING	Martin Locker and Charles Lyons
LAYOUT	Tor Westman
COVER	Andreas Nilsson

Arktos.com   fb.com/Arktos   @arktosmedia   arktosmedia

CONTENTS

Foreword ix

CHAPTER I
Signs of Change 1

CHAPTER II
Retroculture 11
- What is Retroculture? 11
- Breaking away from "Selfism" 12
- A Dialogue with the Past 14
- Bringing the Generations Together 16
- A Change of Lifestyle 17
- Freedom of — and from — Fashion 18

CHAPTER III
Getting Started 25

CHAPTER IV
Retro-Homes 39
- Older Houses 40
- New Homes 43
- "Turning Back the Clock" with the Home You Have 46
- Retro-Interiors 51
- Retro-Neighborhoods 54
- Retro-Homes in Retrospect 57

CHAPTER V
Retro-Families   59

    Starting a Retroculture Family: Dating 67

    Marrying 69

    Retroculture and School 73

    The Retro-Family and Church 76

    Living the Retro Life Alone 79

    Retroculture and Your Life 83

CHAPTER VI
Retro-Clothing   85

    Dressing Up 86

    The Retro Look 87

    New Old Clothes 88

    Retro Accessories 90

    Retro-Shopping, or Making a Chore a Pleasure 93

    Period Clothing: Going All the Way 95

    Amazing Grace 97

CHAPTER VII
Retro-Entertainment   99

    Retro-Television 102

    May I Have This Dance? 105

    Shall We Have a Musicale? 107

    Entertaining at Home 109

    "Johnny, You Must Learn to Entertain Yourself" 115

    Period Entertainments 117

CHAPTER VIII
Retro-Manners   121

    The Golden Rule 123

    Must We Then Act "Hoity-Toity?" 124

Where Do Retro-Manners Apply? 125
Are Retro-Manners Just "Victorian"? 126
Difference Without Disrespect 127
Public Manners. 130
Office Etiquette 133
Which Retro-Manners? 134

CHAPTER IX
Retro-Travel   137
The Train 139
First Class "Plus" 141
Urban Travel: The Second Coming of the Trolley Car. 143
Motoring 149
Walking and Bicycling 153

CHAPTER X
Retro-Business   157

CHAPTER XI
Retro-Service   167
Retro-Service Is Good Business 170
Offering Retro-Service 170
Serving the "Public Good" 172

CHAPTER XII
Retro-America   177

Foreword

WHAT'S GONE IS GONE. You have to keep moving forward. There's no turning back. You can't stand in the way of progress. You can't live in the past.

Everyone has heard these sayings and a hundred others like them. But recently, the tone of voice people use when they say them has begun to change. They used to say them calmly, matter-of-factly, perhaps with a slight chuckle, the way you would tell a child that he really can't fly like Peter Pan. Now, the tone of voice is defensive, insistent, like a person who is trying to keep someone else from blurting out an awful secret.

We are told we must not doubt progress. Still, the growing number of people who are comparing the last few decades to what came before can't help suspecting that somehow, life was better then. We catch glimpses of how it used to be: an old song from the fifties or the thirties on the radio; a black and white photo of a big city street in years past, without potholes or garbage or slums; a beautiful dress from someone's attic; a suburb where the trolley line used to run, with big trees and sidewalks and front porches and people outside talking to their neighbors.

People are noticing these things, and wondering. But we still get the feeling we shouldn't talk about them. If we do, we're told, more harshly, that doubting progress is bad. You must keep moving forward. You have to keep trying things that haven't been done before. Terrible things will happen if instead you try to do what people did in your grandparents' day. You don't want to give up modern medicine, do you? You don't want to go back to Jim Crow racial prejudice, do you? Do you want children working twelve hours a day in dark factories?

The answer is, of course not. But we're still not sure how most of what our grandparents did made the world so terrible. We don't remember them being against good health. We never noticed that they went out of their way to be mean to people. In fact, we thought they were pretty nice. And some things are better now. Most people live longer, and some groups of people have more freedom. That's all good.

So, what is it that attracts us when we catch a glimpse of how people used to live? It's summed up in a word that didn't even exist fifty years ago. That word is lifestyle.

We get the feeling we have forgotten a lot about how to live. We have "home entertainment centers," but our grandparents seemed to find life more interesting. We can get anywhere fast on jumbo jets, but they got to see more from the window of the train. We have email and texting, but people in the old movies talk so elegantly, and we can still enjoy reading the beautifully written letters grandmother saved, letters written by ordinary people. We may have more "leisure time," but they seemed less rushed, less pressured, less under stress.

And amazingly, those older lifestyles often had a lot less impact on the environment. People knew less about the dangers of chemicals and plastics and poisons, but they used a lot less of those things too — sometimes none at all. They didn't need as much energy as we do. They didn't consume as much — or waste as much. They knew how to reuse many things long before the word recycling was ever heard.

When all is said and done, we seem to have lost a lot that was really worthwhile in the last five decades or so. It's not surprising that we yearn to have some of it back again. Nor is it wrong. We know, when we think about it, that it should be possible to recapture the good things people used to do — without giving up modern medicine or sending kids to work in sweatshops.

Much of what we used to have is still around, in bits and pieces here and there. We come across it every day: comfortable, well-built old houses, nice old ways of dressing and talking, old courtesies we find refreshing. Why can't we gather these things up and rebuild the best of what used to be? Why can't we restore old lifestyles the same way people are restoring gracious old houses?

The answer is, we can. And when we look around, we begin to see that a growing number of people are doing it.

JOHN J. PATRICK

CHAPTER I

Signs of Change

VERY OFTEN, the most obvious things are the hardest to see.

At the end of a long, dreary, dismal winter, we are all eager for spring. Then, sometime around March or early April a new day dawns, with a fresh smell in the air, a new warmth, and a powerful sense of quickening life. It's spring, and no one can mistake it.

But long before the first real day of spring, signs of the change in seasons are showing. The first green shoots pop up under the snow. Branches of forsythia take on a hint of color. Country people see these signs, but most of us miss them. Laden down with our daily cares and burdens, we do not notice spring is coming until, suddenly and gloriously, it is upon us.

So it is also with greater changes. Here and there, signs pointing to something new spring up independently. Most of us do not notice them. We do not "connect the dots" to see the outline of the future they portend.

Such signs are now appearing, in places like Medina, Ohio. Like many other small towns in the mid-west, Medina was mostly built in the late-19th century and the first years of the 20th. Its Victorian buildings were grouped around a central square of trees and green lawn, along with a statue or two and a small fountain. Over the years, some of the buildings had become run down. Others had been modernized with metal and plastic facades and signs. A few had been torn down; one corner of the square faced a modern gas station. To most people's eye, the town had nothing special to distinguish it.

But as early as 1967, some Medina citizens began looking at their town through a different eye. They saw it as it once had been, in, say, 1910. They imagined what it might have been like to go to an ice cream social on the square in that year. The buildings were new, clean, and handsome. They reflected the elegant style of the Victorians in their arched windows, elaborate cornices and mansard roofs. They realized that once upon a time, Medina had been a beautiful town. They knew it could be so again.

So the people of Medina turned back the clock. They formed a citizens' group called the Community Design Committee and set out to return Medina to its turn of the century appearance. They fixed up the buildings that had become run down, restoring them, not modernizing them. They stripped the ugly modern facades and signs off the old buildings that had acquired them. They tore down the gas station, and in its place built a Victorian bank so well designed that an observer has no clue that it was built in the 1980s, not the 1880s. They engaged Amish carpenters to build a Victorian bandstand on the square.

If you visit Medina on a Friday evening in the summertime, you will usually find a band playing in the bandstand. Around it are gathered Medina's citizens, listening to turn of the century tunes and enjoying an ice cream social.

What happened in Medina is happening in a growing number of American communities. Instead of tearing down or modernizing old buildings, people are preserving and restoring them. They are turning back the clock.

Telluride, Colorado, is another Victorian town. As in Medina, the old buildings have been restored and the town again looks and feels as it might have in the 1890s. But Telluride has gone even further: all new buildings must be in a Victorian style. Real estate developers have joined in the new movement with enthusiasm. As one article on the town puts it, in Telluride, "developers have a fervor for the past."

Big cities, too, are joining in the effort to preserve and restore their history. Citizens' commissions in many cities have been empowered to channel and guide development to preserve local history. They insist that old buildings be preserved in their appearance, even as they are converted to new uses. In Washington, D.C., not only are famous government buildings like the Capitol protected, so are many 19th-century commercial buildings. Some Washington streets are rapidly recovering their 19th-century appearance.

There are other signs of a change in season. One is Seaside, Florida. In recent years, his Royal Highness the Prince of Wales has become Britain's most noted architectural critic. Perhaps surprisingly, one of his favorite new towns is in America: Seaside, Florida. Seaside was designed from the beginning to have the feel of an American seaside community of the past. Houses are required to have porches, gazebos and pavilions are scattered throughout the town, and everyone has a picket fence. Seeing Seaside as a prototype for new communities built to look and feel like old-fashioned small towns, Prince Charles wrote:

> People will say, 'It's all very well for those with money…' But I believe that the lessons they've worked out at Seaside have very serious applications both in rural areas and in our cities. The founders certainly believe that a sense of real community will grow here; that people will live here. I wish them well.[1]

The architects who designed Seaside, Andres Duany and Elizabeth Plater-Zyberk, a husband and wife team, have proposed more than

---

[1] "Poundbury," an urban extension of Dorchester in Dorset, UK, has since been built along the guidelines laid down by Prince Charles in "A Vision for Britain" (1989). The premise was to favor traditional and new-classical architectural styles, period features, and a rejection of suburban development patterns and zoning. Prince Charles has long been an advocate of traditional architecture and community management, as well as other anti-modern aesthetics and customs. — Editor.

thirty new towns built along historical lines, some of which have been built. *Time* magazine wrote of their work:

> It seems incredible that such a simple, even obvious premise—that America's 18th and 19th century towns remain marvelous models for creating new suburbs—had been neglected for half a century. ... Today Duany and Plater-Zyberk ... and their allies are proposing to go all the way, to build wholly new towns and cities the way our ancestors did.

Architects Larry Garnett and Associates are offering plans for new houses built to a style that suggests the 1920s and 1930s. One such is the "Hampshire." With a steeply sloped, long roof, quaint dormers and a stone-framed entryway, the "Hampshire" suggests both the English countryside and American homes of eighty or ninety years ago. An important fact about this house is that it is not just for the wealthy. With just 717 square feet, it is not a large house, and is affordable to build.

Other firms are offering updated house plans from earlier eras, Victorian through to colonial. Moreover, many new housing developments include such houses. You can often recognize them by their large, comfortable front porches. The front porch had almost completely disappeared from new houses by the 1950s. But more and more people now want what a big porch offers: a place for the family to gather and talk, away from the television and the computer but close to the neighbors and passers-by, who can join in the conversation easily and informally. The front porch serves the trend toward a life oriented more toward people and less toward machines.

Ralph Lauren has become one of America's foremost interior designers. For several years, his interiors have looked strongly toward the past. They are intended to give a feel of life in the 1930s, 40s, and 50s. Why? Because those were times when home life was strong and comforting. He makes heavy use of artifacts from those periods—signs, advertisements, toys and the like—as well as traditional fabrics and furniture designs. His rapidly growing popularity and influence attest to the fact that Americans want to look to the past as they move into the future.

Advertisements and marketing often herald a major change in fashion. More and more ads are now hearkening back to the past. An advert for Hendrick's Gin makes extensive use of aesthetics and themes from the 1920s and 30s, as well as harking back to the days of the British Empire. The Jennings Motor Group has recently launched a project in which several modern cars from Audi, Mercedes and Ford are given retro makeovers, and presented in their ads in a retro style. The ad agencies and designers are clearly on to the same thing Ralph Lauren has discovered: the past sells. People want to buy products that remind them of the past and that take them back into an earlier time. Advertisers sense a change in taste and style, away from a cold, ultra-modern look toward warm, traditional materials, looks and feelings. People are willing to pay to recover some of their heritage.

Traditional styles of dressing are making a major comeback. Men are again wearing double-breasted brown suits with floral ties and even two-toned shoes in some cities. Several online stores are catering specifically to the Retroculture crowd, offering every style from the 1920s right up to the 1950s and early 1960s. One of the most popular of these stores is Unique Vintage, whose clothes are new (rather than second hand) and offer a variety of collections for women. The J. Peterman Company's catalogue stresses the heritage look of many of its products: the Gatsby Pants, the 1950s Tie-Front Blouse and the 1903 Vintage Cologne are all examples of this shift towards "Retro-chic" in fashion. In Britain, the brand 20th Century Chap offers a range of classic British styles from the early part of the last century, with collections focusing on the pre-WWII look and the 1940s.

Clothing styles are a major part of fashion, and more and more they are pointing toward the past. People are buying clothes that suggest earlier times because they like the feeling of those times: the elegance, the suggestion of manners and civility, the return of the idea of "ladies" and "gentlemen," instead of "male" and "female" (and those sometimes hard to tell apart). Men's hair is getting shorter, too, while a recent ad for women's hair stylists speaks of the "Retro look: Finger waves,[2] just like those popular in the 1930s, that are making a comeback." "Unisex" is clearly "out," and the blow-dryers have gone to the attic.

Entertainment is showing a move back toward the past, with movies such as *The Great Gatsby* doing very well in the box offices and reviving interest in the aesthetics of the period. A look back is evident more broadly in movies as well: more and more films resemble those of the "classic" movie era — the 1930s, 40s and 50s — in plot, acting style and look.

The major networks are also discovering the new audience for what is coming to be known as "retro television." The popular AMC series *Mad Men*, which follows the lives of several men working for an advertising company in 1950s and 1960s New York, not only received huge viewing figures but also re-introduced a generation to the style, swing and sophistication of the clothing and culture of 1950s America. A similar story can be found with the HBO series *Boardwalk Empire*, set in the Prohibition era, which revels in the aesthetics of the period.

Train travel is also making a comeback. Amtrak's trains are packed, especially in the summer months, as more and more Americans discover the pleasures of riding the train. Trains enable people to see the country, not just fly over it. The train cuts through all the little towns and cities — often right through people's back yards. It offers unsurpassed views of America's famous sights — the Rocky Mountains, the Hudson River, the Great Plains. In the dining car you can relax over coffee or steak and watch the country roll by. In a car on the interstate, you're lucky to see more than the radiator of a truck in your rear-view

---

2   A hairstyle featuring S-shaped undulations on a relatively bobbed cut, popular in the 1920s and 30s, which made a comeback in the 90s due to its use in the "hip-hop" scene. It has since recently returned in 2016 within certain fashion circles. — Editor.

mirror. An article published on July 18, 2018 in *The Daily Mail* revealed that Amtrak is bringing back their glass-domed observation car on two more routes, the first running through Brunswick, Portland and Boston, and the second through Montreal, Albany and New York. This is a great indicator of the success of the company in the modern era, and the desire by people for this kind of "Retro travel." The train offers many of the things people will be looking for in the future — a slightly slower, more relaxed pace of living, community with other people and places, and a chance to look outward rather than inward.

Classic "motoring" is also coming back. People have already discovered the pleasures of an old way to get around, with several cars from the early 21st century capturing the spirit and aesthetic of "Retro" driving. The 2015 Ford Mustang, the BMW Z8, the revived Mini Cooper and several of the Jaguar sports cars all hark back to the vintage age of motoring, without sacrificing modern comforts and engines. Not to mention the array of "kit cars" which allow people to build their own, with many models mimicking the most well-known classic cars.

Young people, especially young families, are going to church again. Starting in the 1960s, the last place many young people wanted to be seen was in church. "Liberation" was then the latest fashion, and the Ten Commandments were one of the things young people wanted to be liberated from. So, for that matter, were families. The fashion in the 1960s and 70s was "relationships," temporary arrangements for "living together," not marriage. Sad experiences, in the form of broken homes, children raised without parents' love, and lonely people, have made some of today's young people wiser. Families and marriage are coming back. Many young families (and some single people too) want to do things that strengthen their attachment to older, proven, solid ways of living. Going to church is one of those things. And so is belief in God. Far from being unfashionable, belief in God is something more and more young people are open about and look for in others.

The list of old-fashioned things people are finding fun to do is growing daily. More mothers are staying home to take care of their children and getting together with other women in their neighborhood who are doing the same thing. Families are finding board games and puzzles good alternatives to the television or the computer for family entertainment. Family-oriented amusement parks, which were big in the 1890s through the 1930s, have made a tremendous comeback through places like King's Dominion.

In London, a growing group of young people are resurrecting the 1940s — the American 1940s. An article in *The New York Times* reported as early as the 1990s that:

> For many young Londoners, Saturday night is a time to 'rave,' to wear the latest fashions, to dance to the latest hit songs. But just off Leicester Square, young women in smart square-shouldered crepe dresses and open-soled, wedge-soled shoes and men in dapper double-breasted suites and two-toned shoes gather at Fortissimo, a basement club. ... This small but ardent group, mostly in the their 20s and 30s, wear 1940s clothing meticulously, dance the jitterbug expertly and listen to swing, boogie-woogie and early rhythm and blues records religiously. Some embrace 1940s social values and live in homes appointed with 40s furniture, appliances and bric-a-brac.

In certain fashionable areas of the city, especially the Bloomsbury area, there are now a plethora of these "vintage"-style bars, often offering various classic or retro cocktails, radio-play evenings and dance-sessions with the old dances.

Some of the young people involved in this new 40s lifestyle spoke about its inclusion of values and behavior. "People valued things and people a little more," according to a Miss Celia Dunlop. At 1940s clubs, "Guys will put your coat on for you, ask you to dance and see you back to your chair. It's a different attitude. Guys are more respectful. They don't treat you like a piece of meat... In this day and age, it's nice to go back to old values." Mr. Simon Owen added that those values "have become more important. ... On the 40s scene, it's very civilized, very social. There's never any fights. And girls are treated like girls." Mr. Jody Gannon said, "Today, everything's cheap rubbish. Nothing compares to entertainment in the 40s." Young people today, he added, realize "they're being ripped off. They always wear such nasty scowls, as if they hate the world they're in. In the 40s, people had a better attitude about life in general. They didn't clog up their mind with rubbish."

Some people are already going beyond individual old-fashioned activities. They are adding all these activities up and finding that they can amount to a whole new lifestyle, a lifestyle that looks to the past for inspiration. These people are consciously modelling the way they live on the way their grandparents or great-grandparents lived.

One of the most dramatic pieces of evidence for this trend to lifestyles that look to the past — a big change from the ultra-modern — is *Victoria* magazine.

Victoria magazine is devoted to Victorian living, but it is a magazine for modern people — modern people who want a Victorian lifestyle, promising a "return to loveliness." It features articles on interior decoration, clothing and fabrics, gardens, foods, museums — on everything a person needs to give his or her life a Victorian feel. The articles published in the Summer of 2018 include "Cultivating a Love of Antiques," "Preserving Past Grandeur," "The Etiquette of Calling Cards" and similarly themed essays.

Victoria is a glossy, expensive, well-written and well-illustrated magazine, with ads from major companies and a circulation of 800,000. It shows how rapidly the move to past lifestyles is spreading and growing. More and more people are taking a new look at the Victorian age — not just at its clothing and furniture, but at the way of life of the Victorians, with their strong families, solid homes and strong morals. They want to recreate that world in their own lives.

Similar moves to recover past ways of life are evident for other eras. One looks toward the era of the Civil War. It began with the re-creation by volunteers of Civil War military units, which meet to re-enact Civil War battles. That created a market for reproductions of

Civil War uniforms, tents, and other military equipment. Then, the families of the volunteers started to participate in their activities, and a market developed for civilian clothing and accessories. Now, there is a whole "support network" for those interested in the 1860s, with mail-order houses, journals, and magazines like *Civil War Times*.

Of course, none of this means getting rid of modern medicine, cooking every night over an open fire, or watching out for hostile Indians. Rather, the object is to re-create the "feel" of a certain period. After all, people have been doing this for years with colonial style homes and furniture. What we may see is a broadening to include more aspects of lifestyle, such as clothing, cooking (doing so from antique recipes is a growing fashion), reading 18th- or 19th-century literature and listening to period music, and also recovering the moral values of those times. Each individual or family will decide for itself how far it wants to go. But all will be inspired by a vision of the future that includes a recovery of the past.

Architecture, clothing, interior decoration, entertainment, activities, even basic lifestyles, are all looking toward the past in the early 21st century. Is it all just nostalgia? Or is something more happening here — something big?

CHAPTER II

Retroculture

THE ANSWER IS THAT SOMETHING BIG IS HAPPENING. These revivals of past styles are signs pointing to the next change in how Americans live. They point to the "next wave" — the big idea that will shape the 21st century. What is it?
Retroculture.

WHAT IS RETROCULTURE?

Retroculture is a rediscovery of the past and the good things it has to offer. More, it is a recovery of those good things, so we may enjoy them as our parents, grandparents, and great-grandparents enjoyed them. Retroculture rejects the idea that "You can't go back." What we have done before, we can obviously do again. For many years, Americans lived in a land that was safe, solid and comfortable, a civil and even graceful society where life for the overwhelming majority was both pleasant and good. What worked for them can work for us. We can recover the good things they had and knew.

Conventional wisdom says we have no choice but to drive blindly onward into an undefined but increasingly threatening future. Retroculture replies, "Hold on a minute." We do have a choice. Through a dialogue with the past, we can shape that future. We can find ways, by looking back, to make the future promising rather than threatening. We can regain control of our destiny. And in the process, we can reunify the generations instead of pitting one age group against another.

Retroculture reverses the trend this country has been following since the mid-1960s. "Old is bad, new is good" has been the watchword of the last five decades. And it has ended up in a mess. Now, Americans from every walk of life are saying "Enough!" Life yesterday was better in a great many ways than life is today. The time has come to recapture the good things Americans had and have lost. The future can be better than the past—provided we look to the past for guidance.

BREAKING AWAY FROM "SELFISM"

Americans are realizing that the time has come to free themselves from the unhealthy fascination with "self" that has become almost an addiction since the 1960s. "Selfism,"—making the self the focus of life—goes back much further, but traditional moral values always held it in check. Traditional values told us to put service above self. They taught us that happiness comes from disciplining and mastering the rapacious demands of the self, not giving in to them. American culture expected people to focus their lives outward, to do useful things and help other people. It regarded "me first" as a sign of childishness—and of a spoiled child at that.

The flower children of the late 1960s turned these traditional values upside-down. They had the amazingly naive idea that a new "youth culture" could make the world perfect by ignoring "what other people think" and encouraging young people to do whatever felt good whenever they felt like doing it.

"Do your own thing!" became the battle cry of the hippies. Of course, your own thing mustn't be anything your parents or grandparents might do. If possible, it had to be something they wouldn't like at all. Hippies had to be hip, and that meant cutting themselves off from the ideas and standards of older people—except for a few older hip gurus like Timothy Leary or Alan Ginsberg. "Don't trust anyone over thirty," the youth culture advised. Get rid of all the garbage you've been taught. Drop out of the world of families, schools, and workplaces. "Get in touch with your feelings."

But self-discovery, self-realization, and self-fulfillment didn't make life any better. They often made it worse. Youth communes that were supposed to blaze the way to a perfect society instead fell apart because members had no sense of loyalty to the group or to each other. Widely publicized "alternate lifestyles" turned out to be fads, their followers soon growing bored and wandering off. It seemed that however much the self was given it always wanted more. A new pleasure worked a couple of times, then it was dead, and something more extreme had to follow to keep the ever-demanding self "feeling good."

By the mid-1990s almost everybody realized that self-indulgence was not going to save the world or even make it better. But by then, the habit of "selfism" had become too strong to break. Besides, there wasn't much else left. The youth culture of the 60s and early 70s may not have produced anything of lasting value, but it managed to trash the ideals of self-restraint and respect for the wisdom of the ages.

So, the youth culture became "thirty-something" as the baby-boomers drifted through the mindless, feel-good glitter of the disco scene and on into the 1990s. The 90s completed the work of the 60s. With the self still in the driver's seat, things — possessions and image — became the new road to self-fulfillment. Doing your own thing became doing whatever it took to get the trappings of wealth, power and status. In the process, modesty, honesty and fair dealing followed all the other old values onto the scrap heap.

That didn't work either, of course. We still couldn't keep up with the demands of the self, no matter how hard we worked to further our career, get seen in the right places, and pile up designer stuff. "Dressing for success," "winning by intimidation," and keeping score in terms of possessions didn't satisfy us any more than "liberation" and "feeling good." Paper profits melted in the following recession.

Personal debt piled up. Houses and cars and boats became sources of worry rather than satisfaction.

Selfism, it seems, has run head-on into the wall of reality and gone splat. Now, in the 21st century, people are looking back to the times before the wreck. For many young Americans, it seems that the last people they remember being really content were their grandparents. The last time life was good was the 1950s, when most things were still done the old way.

A national poll, taken as early as 1992, showed how people were even then looking back fondly toward the past. 49% thought life in the past was better than it is today; only 17% thought it was worse. 47% felt that their grandparents' lives were happier than their own; only 29% felt they were not as happy. 56% had a generally favorable impression of the Victorian period. A whopping 58% of those polled thought that our nation's political leaders should be leading us back towards the way we used to be.

A DIALOGUE WITH THE PAST

Americans today communicate with a far wider variety of people than ever before, or at least so it seems. Social media, Skype and email connect us to others around the world. We travel to other countries, we go out for Thai or Vietnamese or Caribbean dinners, we see foreign films and drive foreign cars. CNN keeps us up on the very latest news from all around the world.

But there is a large group of people with whom we communicate little, if at all: the Americans who lived before us. And what stories they have to tell! We have more in common with them than with almost anyone else. After all, they lived where we live, saw many of the same scenes we see, and faced many of the same problems.

True, they are no longer with us. But they left us a great many messages, in books and family letters, in the houses and towns they built, and in the furniture, clothes and music they created. In fact, they left us a large sample of the things that made up their daily lives.

And they also left us their thoughts: the values and beliefs they held, ideas of how to live and the reasons to live that way, and memories of specific people — sometimes from our own families — memories that tell us why their lives were respected and even revered by those they touched.

Through the things they left behind we can talk with those who have gone before us. The dialogue can add great richness to our own lives. The immensely popular PBS television series *The Civil War*[3] gave Americans a sense of what a dialogue with the past can offer. Seldom has a television series gripped so many people's emotions so powerfully. Why? Because in it Americans from the past spoke directly to us.

The series had no dialogue between actors. Instead, it presented the words of the people who lived over 100 years ago in many of the same places where we live now. They spoke to us through their diaries, their letters home, their personal photographs. They spoke to us not as names in history books, but as real people struggling with real problems, and we realized that they have a great deal to say to us.

In discovering our own past in people and how they lived, not just in dry facts, we can take a fresh look at ourselves and our own lives. We can learn from their experience. We can find out how they protected themselves from life's harsh blows through the warmth and mutual support of strong families. We can learn how they educated themselves and find that in many ways they were better educated than we are, even if they did not know how to use a computer or a smartphone. We can discover how, with much less wealth and fewer possessions than we have, they managed to build lives we often envy.

We realized in watching *The Civil War* that our own past, the past that earlier Americans lived, has become stranger to us than the

---

3 This was a highly popular mini-series on the Civil War directed by Ken Burns and broadcasted in 1990. The viewing figures were enormous, with roughly 39 million viewers tuning in to any one episode. The series has since been digitally restored and re-released on DVD in 2015. — Editor.

African bush or the Amazon rain forest ever were to them. And we realized at the same time that this need not be so. The past is there, waiting for us to uncover it. We can read the words of those who are gone. And we can also learn from the many people still alive today who remember how people lived before America rejected its inheritance. The enduring pleasures of Retroculture lie in coming home to what is ours.

BRINGING THE GENERATIONS TOGETHER

One writer noted that World War II was the last time when all the generations enjoyed the same music. In the 30s and 40s, kids, parents, and grandparents all sat by the radio listening to Glenn Miller and the Andrews Sisters, "Moonlight Serenade" and "Putting on the Ritz." By the end of the 60s, that kind of sharing between the generations was strictly out. Youth had to do things that were new and that their elders disapproved of. Now, people are wondering, is there anything that can last, anything good enough that people can enjoy it together from generation to generation?

Of course, every era has a certain amount of silliness and false starts. But time is a great filter. Through it passes only the things that are good enough to last. When we look back through that filter, we do not dwell on the flagpole sitters and goldfish swallowing of the 20s or the Zoot suits of the 40s. We dwell on the sound values of the Victorians, the elegant manners at the turn of the century, the classic cars of the 30s and the classy clothes of Fred Astaire.

And all the generations see the same things. Young and old stand together behind time's filter, receiving together the things that have stood its test. Retroculture is not generational; the good things that come to us from the past come to all of us together. All, young and old, can again enjoy Glenn Miller. Everyone can admire a Victorian town restored to its original appearance. For the first time in generations, we can all sing from the same sheet of music — quite literally.

Retroculture also restores the link between living generations. Our grandparents can tell us what it was like to travel in the great days of the railroads, with steam engines, Pullman cars, crystal and heavy silver in the dining cars. They can show us the places they loved. They can have the joy of teaching, of transmitting to their descendants their experiences, their wisdom, their lives. Young people, in turn, can again have the excitement of discovering things through their own family and friends, including friends from other generations. They can learn of many pleasures they would never know if they relied only Facebook and Twitter as their guides. They can be the true heirs of those who went before them, receiving and treasuring things of lasting value.

Many young people today are becoming admirers of old houses, especially Victorian and turn of the century homes. We can tour some that are now museums, seeing their beautiful craftsmanship, the fine woodwork and stained glass, and furnishings that speak of a rich and close family life. But how much more it means when the fine old house belongs to someone who is willing to share the life that went on in that house: how great-grandfather used to preside at the dinner table, how grandmother as a child used to wait for the iceman to catch a few cold slivers on a summer day. These things reach across the generations and bring us together again.

The decades that we have been apart have lasted too long. Children and parents and grandparents have lived them out finding life meager and lonely, cut off from one another in separate worlds. Retroculture offers things in common. The past—the same past—is open to all. Each has a role to play, some teaching, some learning. Through Retroculture, the 21st century will be a time for bringing the generations back together.

A CHANGE OF LIFESTYLE

How do we recover the good things our grandparents had? The slower life, time for hobbies, family and interests, less rampant consumerism in our daily lives? The answer is Retroculture's little secret. What is it? We get there by living as they did—by adopting a Retroculture lifestyle.

Of course, this does not mean we return to the past in everything. We will not give up modern medicine (even the Amish go to doctors), junk the furnace and the air conditioner, or keep slaves. Each person will be free to decide how "Retro" he wants to live; some will want to go farther than others, and no one is "wrong" for only going far enough to give their life the degree of old-fashioned feeling they want. But more and more, Americans will be modelling their lifestyle on the way people lived in the past.

FREEDOM OF — AND FROM — FASHION

In fact, freedom is one of the most important characteristics of Retroculture. Not only do you choose just how Retro you want to live, you also "pick your own time." This is nothing less than a revolution in the whole notion of "fashion."

Retroculture is itself a fashion, in the large sense of the word. But it is also freedom to choose your own fashion. Up until now, fashion was always a tyrant. At any given time, only one style of clothing, music, dancing, architecture, interior design, furniture, entertainment, manners and even values were considered "in fashion." Unless you conformed to that one fashion, you were "out of it." People saw you as stodgy and out-of-date if you stayed behind the fashion—or radical and weird if you got too far ahead of it. Either way, fashion said that something was wrong with you.

Retroculture breaks the tyranny of fashion. People who look to the past for models are "in fashion" for the time they have chosen, but other people who have chosen a different period are equally in fashion, even though to outward appearances the two fashions may be completely different. People who model their lifestyles after different periods will obviously differ from each other in the sort of clothes they want to wear, the music they want to hear, the way they keep themselves entertained, the houses they live in and the furniture they use. But each group will be "in fashion" for the period it is reviving and none of these periods will be "out of fashion." No Retroculture period is "wrong." Further, each Retro group can enjoy and appreciate what other groups are doing.

The freedom to "pick your own period" and live it to the extent you want is important because different times appeal to different people. Yet all Retroculture people have something very important in common. They all look beyond the self-gratification and accumulation of possessions that have driven the last few decades. So they all look to the past, to times when people's lives had a better focus, and they find that the past offers many different and equally interesting fashions to choose from.

Is there a "cut-off point" for Retroculture, a date too far back for a lifestyle to be at all practical or one so recent that it can't really be thought of as Retro? There is no arbitrary cut-off point, although it is obviously easier today for someone to live as they might have in 1940 or even at the turn of the century than to adopt a style of living from the colonial period. On the other hand, because Retroculture is an effort to recapture the good things Americans had and did before the 1960s made it fashionable to throw those things away, the 1950s are probably the last years that offer much in the way of a model for Retro living. The rootless rebellion, shallow hedonism, and ruthless materialism that followed do not. We know where the last decades have led us. That is what the Retro movement wants to get away from.

The most important thing about Retroculture is not where it draws the line, but how much it offers: the post-World War II era, with its energy and optimism; the 1930s, when tough times led people back to what matters most — strong families, honest work and helping the less fortunate; the excitement of the Roaring Twenties, when young people, especially, knew how to have fun; farther back to the Victorian period and the creation of great American cities and magnificent houses; even back as far as the colonial period, the first distinctly

American lifestyle. Fashion no longer dictates that we can only have some furniture from colonial times, maybe a vintage car from the 1930s, or perhaps a few rock-and-roll records from the 50s. All of America's past, in all of its richness, lies open to those who choose to live it.

What might it be like to live in the Retro years? Let's look ahead a bit — say, to the year 2030 — when the trends that we see starting now have had time to develop and spread. How might people be living then?

Bill and Mary Brunelli are both in their early thirties and have two children, eight and ten. They love the elegance of the late 1800s, so that is how they choose to live. They own a Victorian house built in 1897 in a small town outside Cincinnati, Ohio. The house was in bad shape when they bought it. Its former owners had schlocked it, trying to "modernize" it by stripping off the gingerbread and putting in picture windows and aluminum siding.

The Brunellis researched the house and found photos from before the remodeling. They got a lot of useful advice from the local Restoration Society, a volunteer group who are working to restore the town's Victorian flavor. They read about the dos and don'ts of Victorian restoration in articles from *Old House Journal*. They even talked with an old man from the neighborhood who had grown up in the house and remembered much more than what they could find out from the records. With the help of local craftsmen who have relearned traditional skills, from carpentry to plastering, the Brunellis brought their home back to mint condition.

They already had a number of Victorian antiques, and they did not hesitate to add good reproductions from the increasing number of companies that were offering them. *Victoria* magazine and other publications that had sprung up to cater to the growing Retro movement helped them decorate their house like the Victorians, letting them choose from a wide variety of authentic paint colors, wallpaper patterns, and fabrics. They found that many seed and plant catalogues had sections dedicated to period gardens. The side yard became a Victorian rose garden, where Mary can pursue her hobby of growing rare 19th-century varieties of roses and invite friends to tea in the small, white-trellis gazebo.

The Brunelli's sometimes wear late 19th-century clothes as well. They dress "Victorian" for events sponsored by the town's Victorian Society, one of several social clubs that now focus on particular historical periods. They dress that way when they invite friends over for 19th-century dinners on weekends, and sometimes for church or for dinner parties with friends. Although they have a television and a computer, the Brunellis also enjoy period entertainment. At least once a week the family gathers in the parlor and Mary or Bill reads out loud. Light novels from the turn of the century provide plenty of rousing tales for the children, who also like many of the old-fashioned parlor games their parents have taught them.

When they go out walking together, the Brunellis sometimes stop to talk with Mr. and Mrs. Chen, an older couple who now have the freedom to recreate the 1950s lifestyle they enjoyed so much when they were young. When the Chens sold their successful clothing store in Cincinnati and retired to this town several years back, they bought one of the first "ranch-style" houses that had been built in the area. It still had the original knotty pine paneling in the den, although it had to be stripped and varnished to bring back its original warm glow. In the kitchen, they installed rounded "streamlined" kitchen appliances they had rescued from an old house that was being torn down. In the bathroom, they ripped out the wall-to-wall carpeting and laid bright yellow tile from the early 1950s with black tile trim, which they could now order through the local hardware store. They also put in reproduction fixtures with the same round lines as the kitchen appliances.

Most of the Chens' furniture, which they had bought used as newlyweds and lovingly maintained, is already right for the period. It includes an early television, which is now hooked up with a DVD player that lets them watch vintage television shows. Of course, they have a record player for their vinyl collection, but they are glad that first-rate versions of most old hit songs are also available on compact discs for the stereo system they have tucked away out of sight. They have always loved dancing, and they frequently attend the "hops" sponsored by a local dance revival group at the restored ballroom of an old amusement park a few miles out of town, an activity they say is great for keeping fit. Mr. Chen drives one of the reproduction 1948 Buick Roadmasters General Motors now makes for fans of post-World War II design.

When they are not doing repairs or chores around the house, the Chens like to dress the way their parents taught them. Mr. Chen usually wears a three-button blazer or a cardigan sweater with a tie. Mrs. Chen prefers dresses to jeans or shorts. Both of them appreciate the freedom to dress and talk a bit more formally than used to be the fashion, without the neighbors thinking that they are acting stuffy or stand-offish. In fact, they enjoy walking along the street and visiting with the neighbors in the evening, and they find many others doing the same. Even after dark, they feel perfectly safe out walking, now that so many other people are doing it too.

Through their dance revival group, the Chens have become friendly with a young black family from Cincinnati, the Martins. African-American Lateesha Martin is a middle-level manager at city hall. Charlie is a technician at the city water plant. The Martins' real love is swing music, particularly the music of Duke Ellington. Charlie is a good enough trombonist to have made a living as a studio musician for a few years in New York, but the spread of synthetic computer music for movies and television put him out of work, and he returned to Cincinnati and settled down with his hometown sweetheart.

Now Charlie spends many weekends playing the ballroom outside town with the swing band he helped form. He and Lateesha and their two young children often drive out for weekends and visit the Chens, who never had children or grandchildren of their own. All of them go to hear Charlie's band play, and the Chens have been teaching Charlie and Lateesha late-40s dance routines. If the number of swing fans continues to grow, Charlie may even have a chance to become a full-time musician again.

Meanwhile, through their church the Brunellis have gotten to know a young man named Jon Hendrickson, who lives outside town. Jon prefers a colonial lifestyle. He has also chosen to go more Retro than either the Brunellis or the Chens. He bought some land and built a log cabin on it. The cabin comes in kit form, the sort many people have for a summer house, and it's quite comfortable. Importantly for a young man without much money, it is also relatively cheap.

Jon has made much of his own furniture, just as pioneers in the Cincinnati area made theirs in the late 18th century. He has electricity, mainly for his computer — he works out of his home as a graphic designer — and for the kitchen, but those rooms are separated from the rest of the house. The main room of the house is a dining-living-bedroom all rolled into one, just as it would have been in his period, and everything is as it would have been then.

There is a big fireplace, candles for light, a few pieces of furniture, and a table around which people gather to eat, drink, talk, and play cards.

Jon wears only Colonial-style clothes at home, which he orders through catalogs, and he looks good in them. He is convinced that men's dress peaked in the late 18th century, with knee breeches, bright-colored waistcoats, and buckle shoes. John also studies the 18th-century art of deportment. In that time, people were careful how they stood, sat, and gestured, always aiming for elegance. Usually, he speaks modern English, but he belongs to a club where he gathers with others to discuss 18th-century subjects in the English of that time. The group meets at the famous Golden Lamb Inn in Lebanon, Ohio. If you attend one of their meetings, you will feel as if you have traveled back in time.

John's careful re-creation of 18th-century living does not limit him. He drives a car, flies to business meetings, belongs to an HMO, goes to the movies, and enjoys other modern conveniences. But he appreciates the fact that he is free to live in his chosen period without being thought strange. A considerable number of people have chosen Colonial living. It is not uncommon to see people dressed in Colonial clothes — or clothes from any number of other periods — on their way to the numerous events attended by others who have chosen the same period.

At this point, you may be saying to yourself, "This is interesting. After all, in many ways the past was better. But… can we really go back to the past? Is it practical? And isn't this just nostalgia?"

These are natural questions. Answering them is the first step in getting started toward your own Retroculture lifestyle. And they do have answers.

Let's take a look at some of the questions that may have occurred to you and see what the answers are.

CHAPTER III

Getting Started

> "Is it really possible to recreate the past?
> After all, we've been told over and over that
> 'You can't go back.'"

RETROCULTURE DOES NOT attempt to recreate the past precisely. That would require living in a museum. Rather, it attempts to use the past to guide our way into the future. It draws what is good from the past and blends it with what is good in the present, creating a "roadmap" we can follow as we move into the future. It offers a way to shape the future, to recapture control of our destiny — something we cannot do if our only guide is novelty, doing that which has never been done before.

15th-century Europeans gave the world a big boost forward by trying to go back to the ideas and art forms of classical Greece and Rome. We call that time the Renaissance. The Italians who created the Renaissance did not suddenly become ancient Romans again. But they did change the direction their society was taking — and improve it — by looking to the Classical past for guidance.

Similarly, the Protestant Reformation was an attempt to return to what people such as Martin Luther believed was the early Christian church, the church in the first few centuries after Christ.

The Protestants had an enormous impact on Christianity, including, through the Counter-reformation, on the Catholic Church. Both Protestants and Catholics sought to remedy abuses in the church by attempting to go back to their roots.

Neither the Renaissance nor the Reformation exactly recreated the past. Nor will Retroculture. But both did give people a light by which to see and a path to follow into the future. Retroculture can do the same for Americans today. It can give us guidance, inspiration, new ideas (really old ideas rediscovered), and models we can follow. It can allow us to find solutions to current problems by showing us what worked in the past. It can recover many of the qualities of life in America in say, the year 1900, qualities like civility, sound values, strong family life, and neighborhoods, towns and cities that are pleasant places to live.

As to the saying "You can't go back," it is a warning, not against trying to recover the good things from the past — which we can do — but against the people who keep telling us that we can't go back. Very often, these people have selfish interests in present trends. Some are people whose lifestyles might face disapproval if most Americans return to traditional values. Some have financial interests in rampant consumerism, in selling "upscale" goods with "prestige" labels. Some work in industries, such as entertainment, that might have trouble adjusting to Retroculture's recovery of good taste. Most of them fear the rejection of "selfism" inherent in Retroculture, because their own lives are very self-centered.

So, when you hear, "You can't go back," watch out. What the person who tells you that is really saying is, "You can go back, and I'm afraid of what might happen to my interests if you do." Be certain you recognize what that person's interests really are — what his hidden agenda is.

> "A lot of Retroculture seems to be about things — fashions, architecture, furniture, etc. Isn't it too materialistic, just like today?"

Retroculture includes things — clothing, home design, furniture and so on — but it is not about them. They are "props" Retroculture people use to create in their homes and lives the feel of an earlier period. What Retroculture is really about is how life is to be lived, the values, ideas and standards that guide behavior. After all, what made earlier times better than the present was that people behaved differently, not just that their houses or clothes were different.

Traditional American values are, in fact, perhaps the most important thing Retroculture seeks to recapture. If we could bring some Americans from the past, from the Colonial period or the era of the Civil War or the turn of the century, back to visit and talk with us today, they would almost certainly tell us that the most important things in their lives were what they believed.

What were their beliefs? We have touched on many of them already: civility, public spiritedness, charity, craftsmanship and stewardship, among others. But these values in turn were expressions of deeper beliefs, beliefs past Americans got from their religious faith. After all, America was founded by Pilgrims: people who came here seeking freedom to worship as they believed right. Our ancestors, from almost any era, believed in God, worshipped Him regularly, and were molded by their faith and worship.

Their morals were rooted in the Ten Commandments. Like people at all times, they seldom lived up to all of them. But even when they fell short, they still recognized that the Commandments were right. Only in recent years have Americans said, in effect, "If we can't perfectly live up to the rules while doing just what we want to, we'll re-write the rules."

Earlier Americans recognized that the rules — traditional morals — were right. Further, they were necessary: they were the basis of the strong families, sound communities, and productive workplaces those Americans knew and had. Even Americans who were not personally religious usually accepted the Ten Commandments as something right and good.

It would be an error to think we can recover the good things from America's past simply through reviving styles of architecture, clothing, and entertainment. Those are enjoyable, and they are part of Retroculture. But the more important part is reviving the values and morals and religious faith held by the Americans who first created those styles. The one was the form, the other the substance, and we will quickly find the form without the substance is unsatisfying.

Retroculture is, after all, a way of living. Any way of living requires a guide. The guides from the last fifty years, from "do your own thing" through "I've got mine, Jack," have proven false. Retroculture is a call to return to an earlier guide, one that lasted and proved itself by many generations of Americans. Call it what you will—American values, traditional morals, the Ten Commandments or the Jewish or Christian faith—it works. As a guide, it is true. We need it, now more than ever.

"Is it practical to try to live as we did in the past?"

One of the biggest advantages of returning to the past is its practicality. Americans have always been a practical people. In many respects those who went before us lived more simply and practically in their time than we do in ours. Despite the increased pace and distractions of our world—perhaps, in part, because of them—many old ways of living are at least as practical now.

For example, as late as the 1940s, people walked a lot more than they do now. There were fewer cars and more public transit systems. Public transit was clean, orderly, efficient and attractive. So people of all ages rode the subways and trolleys for both business and pleasure, and wherever they got off, they walked. Exercise was a practical part of everyday life, not an added chore.

Today, most of us drive, even though everyone knows that driving a car does nothing to improve our health. But, given a chance, people are amazingly willing to go back to older forms of transportation that include walking. Look at the many American cities that have built Light Rail streetcar lines. Those lines not only carry many people who would not want to ride buses, they re-vitalize the city's downtown by letting people get around without cars. They ride the trolleys, then they get off and walk, bringing new business to local merchants.

Retroculture is also a lot more practical for the environment, one of today's biggest concerns. People traveling in streetcars produce far less pollution and use up much less fuel than they would if they were driving their cars. Only a few decades ago, people had a lot less impact on the environment and nature's limited resources, even though they knew much less about the environment. And they managed to live comfortably, even by our standards.

People got along without buying as many things, and they demanded higher quality in the things that they did buy, so they would last longer and not have to be thrown out. They took the time to fix things, and they had many ways of reusing what was worn out, not because anyone thought much about recycling but because Americans were practical and hated waste.

Ordinary citizens also demanded beauty in the things they purchased. As a result, American consumer goods were among the best designed and best made in the world. Indirectly, this also tended to reduce the burden on the environment, because beautiful and well made things were less likely to be discarded, and many older tools did not require electricity.

"Isn't Retroculture just another word for nostalgia?"

In fact, Retroculture is quite different from nostalgia. Nostalgia looks to an imaginary world, a perfect world that never really was. Usually, that world is represented by an idyllic, innocent rural life. In the nostalgic view, that world can never be recaptured. It is lost forever. Of course it is, since it never really existed in the first place.

Retroculture, in contrast, remembers real past ways of living. The 1950s, the 1920s, the 1890s were all real. None of them was perfect, unlike the imagined world of nostalgia. But all of them had some—indeed, many—good qualities. Retroculture can recapture those good things from earlier periods because they were real. We can cook a Colonial dinner, build a new Victorian house, dance to big band music and live solid, moral, respectable lives because real people did those things. Through memory and history—which is the memory of times before our own—we can find out what people used to do, and we can do those things again. By doing so, we can regain what we had and have lost: contentment, well ordered communities, communication among generations, lives that are rewarding because they are lived according to good standards.

Nostalgia, after all, is really just a feeling. We say that a certain view or picture or song makes us feel nostalgic. It is a bittersweet feeling, a wistfulness or longing. Retroculture, on the other hand, is action. It is the recovery and re-creation of things from the past to make them part of our everyday lives. The actions we take to create a Retroculture lifestyle, from wearing old clothing fashions to going to church, give us good feelings, sometimes even feelings of nostalgia. But Retroculture is more than feelings; it is a way of living.

"But wasn't the past bad?"

Some people may say that it is wrong to try to turn the clock back. "Political Correctness" paints the past as something bad, a dark time of "repression" and intolerance. The Victorian period especially is often portrayed this way. Victorian family life is seen as "uptight," stiff and formal. The Victorians were supposedly often hypocritical, extolling virtues they did not practice. The real Victorians, according to this view, were priggish, snobbish, cold and nasty.

Recently, people have begun to have a more balanced — and more historically correct — view of past times. The Victorian period is increasingly recognized as a time of tremendous creativity and achievement. The Victorian years saw the United States transformed from a fairly primitive, largely agricultural country into a powerful, modern nation. What kind of people undertook such a great transformation? Far from being narrow and unimaginative, they were people of broad vision, tremendous energy, and great ability to innovate. They were inventors and builders, people who could and did remake their world — and ours.

Their strengths began at home, with a strong, close-knit family life. Religion and morals were an important part of family life, as was education. The Victorians were determined to build a better world for their children, starting with a careful upbringing. They were also deeply concerned with improving the communities they lived in. If you look at the many towns and cities the Victorians built, you immediately see that the most imposing buildings are usually the churches. That tells us what the Victorians believed to be most important: the moral, not just the economic future of their communities. Similarly, they put great effort into creating good schools. They founded many "improvement societies," aimed at eliminating drunkenness, helping the poor, Americanizing immigrants, and generally improving community life.

The Victorians and people from other earlier times were not bad people. On the contrary, they had high standards, and most of them tried to live up to those standards. Of course, there are bad people in every era; human nature does not change. But the Victorian period in particular was a time when people spent a great deal of thought and energy trying to be good — and to do good for others.

Retroculture seeks to recapture the good things the Victorians, and those from other times as well, knew and did. The things that were less good Retroculture will pass over. No one seeks to return to Jim Crow laws,[4] 19th-century medicine, or outdoor plumbing. A Retroculture lifestyle will have plenty of room for air conditioning and automobiles.

"If I am the first person in my community to 'go Retro,' won't I feel uncomfortable or even embarrassed?"

You don't have to "go Retro" in any way that makes you uncomfortable in order to be Retro. Just do what you enjoy. For example, if you would feel embarrassed to be among the first people to wear old clothing styles, don't do it. Do something else instead, something less visible to people outside your family, like reviving family Sunday dinner, or listening to old music, or decorating your particular room in your house — your den, your bedroom — to reflect the era you like best.

Remember, Retroculture offers freedom from fashion. You are free not only to choose your era, but also to "get into" it as little or as deeply as you like. Just as you will respect others' decisions about how Retro they want to live, so they will respect yours. After all, the past Retroculture seeks to revive was a comfortable time. It makes sense that in adopting Retroculture, you will control how far you go in it and will do whatever you find comfortable.

---

4 These were the official statuary acts which enforced racial segregation in the US. Their origins can be traced back to 1865, and they stood in place until the mid-1960s. — Editor.

Also, if you look around, you will probably already see other people in your community who are starting to go Retro. A good way to get started is by doing things in groups, just like the young people who are reviving the American 1940s in London, England. Group activities can make everyone more comfortable, and also make Retroculture more fun by allowing people to share their knowledge, talents, and interests with others.

"Isn't Retroculture phony and artificial — something created, rather than something natural?"

As Oscar Wilde said, "The only thing wrong with being natural is that it is such a difficult pose to maintain." The fact is, anything beyond eating raw meat and sleeping in caves is created — a pose, if you will. Civilization itself is something people deliberately create — something "artificial," and, to some people, "phony." But it is also something that most people are very glad we have, since raw meat doesn't taste very good and caves are cold and damp.

Once we agree we prefer civilization over savagery, and thus the created over pure "nature," we have to ask, "Which is more natural, looking to the past for inspiration and guidance or toward novelty as our only guide?" Through most of human history, people looked toward the past, and novelty was suspect. People have naturally preferred the known over the unknowable, and the tried and proven over the novel and untested. It is only in recent years that we have gotten our wires crossed and come to think that it is somehow "phony" to look toward the past and try to revive what used to work. In a time when most people realize that life was, on the whole, better in the past than it is today, what could be more natural than trying to revive it?

"Is Retroculture just another fad?"

There is too much happening in Retroculture for it to be just a fad. Fads are things like hula-hoops and granny dresses, things than cannot last. Already, we see strong Retro influences in such serious fields as architecture and urban planning. We see people devoting substantial time and work to restoring old houses to their original state, to bringing back decaying towns and urban centers, and to local history. We see real commitment to discovering and reviving past ways of living. No fad can produce that kind of seriousness.

Retroculture is a reaction against fads, against living a life that follows one silly novelty after another. It is a return to "the permanent things," to the ways of thinking and ways of living that have defined us, over the generations, as Americans. These things have proven their worth by standing the test of time—a test that quickly separates out the fads and fancies. We have had to endure lives governed by fads and social experiments since the mid-1960s, and now we are saying, "Enough!" It's time to get back to what we know works, and that is just what Retroculture does.

"Does Retroculture require limiting technology?"

Most Retroculture people will want to limit technology. It will be difficult to recover old ways of living if you or your family spend most of their time at home staring at a screen. Of course, your work may require you to use a computer or a smart phone. But to re-create the era you want, in your home life you will probably try to put modern technology in its place. Most people now see that it has come to dominate and control our lives in ways that are not healthy. Think of your home as a place that gives you a "vacation" from all the devices that constantly fight for your attention with their "bings and bongs." One of the nicest things about the old days was their quiet.

Once you have answered your questions about Retroculture, you face making a decision. Do you want to lead a Retrocultural life? Do you want to use the past as your guide and inspiration as you move into the future? That is a choice only you can make. And it is a serious choice, even if it is a choice about doing something that can be a great deal of fun.

Perhaps the best way to make this choice is to ask yourself two questions. The first is: "Do you want to take charge of your own life? Do you want to decide where your future will go, and how you will live your life?" Retroculture offers a way you can do this. If you choose the past as your guide, you can determine where you want to go and how you want to live, because you have something real, something knowable to steer by.

The second question to ask yourself is whether you would enjoy being part of Retroculture. Does this sound like fun to you? Would you enjoy being part of a national effort to recover our past and make it live again? Like all real fun, it involves some work and some serious commitment — just like sailing, or quilting, or gardening. But people do those things because they enjoy them. Is this something you would enjoy? Is it something that would give new meaning and purpose and pleasure to your life?

If your answer is "no," we still encourage you to finish this little book. As you look more closely at Retroculture, you may find your answer changing. Many Americans are finding Retroculture fun, and also meaningful and important. Most of them are people who, until recently, would never have considered looking to the past to find good and useful ways to live in America in the 21st century. You may discover what they have found, that the more you look at the past, the more what you see there makes sense.

If your answer is "yes," you may find yourself asking the question, "But how do I get started?" Most of the rest of this book is an answer to that question. But there are a few general suggestions we can offer here that you may find helpful.

The first thing you may want to do is find out more about different periods. You may not yet know what period most interests you, the one you would like to revive in your own life. There are a number of ways to get a feel for different times. Local museums are a good place to start, especially museums in the form of colonial farms or Victorian homes. It can also be useful simply to walk through neighborhoods that are solidly Victorian or say, 1920s–1930s. You will probably find a number of homes there that have been restored to their original appearance. Of course, especially for the colonial period, there are towns such as Williamsburg, Virginia and Plymouth, Massachusetts, that have been restored to their period appearance, with people dressing in colonial styles who will explain life in that time to you. You may want to pay one of those places a visit.

You may find in your local area groups of people with interests in different periods. For example, you may have a local Civil War regiment—people who gather to reenact battles from the Civil War. Or, there may be a local group of people interested in ballroom dancing. Many of them may wear period dress, practice period manners and speech, and know a great deal about the time in which the dances they enjoy were first popular. Groups of this kind will usually welcome your interest in "their" time.

Of course, the local library is always a good starting place. There are many books on life in past periods, from the colonial through the 1950s. Magazines such as *Victoria* may also be found there. Further, local libraries often have material on local history, from books through actual archives of local newspapers and other publications. The history of your city, county, town or neighborhood is often a good place to get started, because a past period may "come alive" more for you when you can see how the place where you live used to be.

One of the best sources of information on past periods is the older generation. Your own grandparents or great aunts and uncles will probably be happy to tell you what life used to be like, especially for your own family—and they will be happy to be asked. Nothing adds quite so much to your house and neighborhood as knowing what it used to be like for your own family. If you now live far from where your family used to live, there will probably still be local senior citizens who can tell you a great deal about what your area was like when they were young. Even if you are in a new development, it may have an older town center with an interesting history, and local people who can remember it. Nothing would so nicely make the day for people in the local senior citizens' center as to have you come by and ask them about "how it used to be." Remember, one of the good things about Retroculture is that it can bring the generations together again.

Once you have a feel for the period you would like to "adopt" as your own, your discovery can get more specific. The more you dig, the more you will find — books, periodicals, local groups of enthusiasts, people who have restored homes, etc. At some point, you will probably want to choose a place to start in "going Retro" yourself. This can be almost anything. Often, people like to begin with the way they decorate their home. Cooking period recipes and serving old-fashioned family dinners is another good starting point. If you like to sew, you can begin with quilting, or making clothes to period patterns, which are readily available through catalogues. Collecting and listening to music from your period, perhaps on original recordings, or learning to play a period instrument is another good point to begin. Or, take up a hobby that reflects the time you like best, such as collecting train models. That is an especially good way to meet other people interested in the same period.

Already, there are a growing number of Retroculture items on the market, from clothing through furniture and appliances to plans for houses. As you find yourself needing something new, you can get it made to a Retro style. Gradually, your home or wardrobe will take on the feel of the period you like. At the same time, you can gradually increase the number of Retro things you do, from taking family drives in the country to giving period dinners for friends to going regularly to church. Each new activity turns back the clock in more of your own life.

The most important thing to remember about getting started on a Retroculture lifestyle is that it is not difficult. On the contrary, it is fun. It is an opportunity to discover new people, learn new things, and find new — really old — ways of living better. Many other people across the country are going to be doing the same thing. As the number of people following a Retro lifestyle grows, new publications, volunteer groups, products and services will come along to serve them. Retroculture will be the wave of the 21st century — it's already starting to happen all around us. Yes, it takes some effort on your part, but everything worthwhile does. That's one of the things the past is waiting to teach us: the deep and lasting rewards that come from something that takes time, work, and commitment. So — let's get started!

CHAPTER IV

∽

Retro-Homes

HOME IS WHERE THE HEART IS, and a great deal more as well. It is our refuge, where the wicked cease to trouble and the weary are at rest. It is the place, more than any other, where we can really be ourselves. For Retro-people, when we have closed the front door behind us, it is where we at last escape the importunities of modern life.

Not surprisingly, the home is the first thing many people want to take Retro. There, we can create the world we desire. Often it is a world we remember: our parents' or grandparents' house, or the special world we found as children in the home of a favorite aunt. If we are fortunate, we may have some of the furniture or pictures or knick-knacks from those homes of memory, tools we can use to re-create their feel.

There is a great deal more to a home than a house, but it is with a house that the Retro-home begins. Fortunately, a wide variety of styles is available, all suitable to Retro-living. From Colonial through Victorian and Queen Anne to the ranch-style houses of the 1950s, you can almost certainly find something to fit your taste and budget.

OLDER HOUSES

In fact, the budget gets some help right off the bat from one simple fact: most Retro-people want older homes. Usually, older homes are less expensive. Look through the real estate section of your local paper. Often you will find nice older homes in established neighborhoods, convenient to town, places with sidewalks and big trees, nearby schools and streetcars, selling for one half or even one third of what new houses cost.

These older homes have what Retro-people are looking for. Depending on their style, they may offer high ceilings, broad front porches, and leaded glass cabinets built into the dining room; solid brickwork, arched doorways, and slate roofs; or broad living rooms that step down into spacious dining areas, wide windows, and big patios. They are built better than houses are today, with thicker studs and more of them, superior masonry (especially brickwork), and real hardwood floors (not even the cheapest houses of 80 years ago had plywood floors disguised by "free wall-to-wall carpet").

Most important, older houses speak of lives lived in earlier and nicer times. That adds something even the best new house, one carefully built to an older style, can never offer. The people who lived in these older homes, in 1880 or 1920 or 1950, have left a bit of themselves and their lives to the people who buy them today. In a time of restless change, that continuity is welcome.

As far as styles go, what is available will depend on where you live. In the East, it is possible in some places to find genuine colonial houses, though unless you are looking in a remote area they are likely to be expensive. More probably, if you're looking for a colonial home, you will want a reproduction. Some very nice Cape Cods and other colonial styles were designed and built in the 1930s, 40s and 50s; they can be found in most parts of the country and often for reasonable prices. Many of these reproductions were small houses, especially suitable to single people, young couples just getting started and families where the children have grown and moved on. Though small, t

CHAPTER IV. RETRO-HOMES

FIGURE 1. Entrance sign to Seaside, Florida.
(Source: M.Fitzsimmons, Wikimedia Commons)

hey are often charming, with imaginative use of space, distinguishing features such as gables, fine interior woodwork and fireplaces, and the feel of much larger and more expensive homes. (Note: some real estate agents now list almost any older home as a "colonial." This is, of course, bogus; if you are looking for an older colonial, you will probably have to spell out to your agent just what a colonial house is.)

One of Retroculture's characteristics is a re-awakened admiration for the Victorians. Not surprisingly, Victorian and Queen Anne houses — homes built from around 1870 to about 1910 — are many people's first choice. And what beautiful homes they often are! The outside features great front porches; stately cupolas; long, elegant windows, often arched at the top; or, in the later Queen Anne[5], a de-

---

5 This Baroque form of 18th-century English architecture was revived in the 19th century, typically formed in a simple yet elegant style, featuring sash windows in boxes, warm fine brickwork, broad porches etc. The American form of this revival is marked by its fine gabling.

lightful excess of scrollwork, whimsical balconies, and as many odd corners and cornices as an architect could dream up. Inside, you may find a wide front hallway, with symmetrical parlors on either side, set off with elaborate fretwork; beautiful paneling, especially around the elegant formal stairway; high ceilings with plaster moldings; stained glass or prism-framed windows; and, instead of a few big rooms, a wide variety of small rooms, each seeming larger than it is through its use of vertical space, and each intended for a specific purpose: the music room, the library, the morning room, the conservatory, and so on. Many people who follow a Retroculture life style want nothing quite so much as one of these enchanting, exuberant homes, so eloquent of America at its peak.

There are few areas of the country that do not have any Victorian or Queen Anne homes. Some places, like the Midwest, have them in abundance. If the houses are in excellent original condition or have been restored well and are in desirable neighborhoods, they are usually expensive. But you may find them at reasonable prices also, by looking in small towns that were built in the latter part of the 19th century, or in areas of the city that have run down. If you are willing to be an "urban pioneer," one of the first people to go into a rundown area and begin restoration, you may be able to get a beautiful Victorian quite cheaply in what will someday become a good neighborhood.

Often one of the best buys in Retro-homes are houses built between 1910 and 1940. These vary widely in style, from Colonial Revival through the bungalows and American Foursquares to neo-Spanish and the Prairie Style inspired by Frank Lloyd Wright. Not yet as fashionable as Victorian or Queen Anne houses, these homes nonetheless offer many of their virtues. They are often marvelously comfortable, with high ceilings, big front porches, elegant interior woodwork and a variety of special-purpose rooms like sunrooms and breakfast rooms. Architecturally, they can be quite distinguished, both in overall form and quality of details. The Colonial Revival in particular improved markedly through this period, by the end of it becoming a nearly-faithful reproduction of genuine Colonial homes.

The bungalow, which slowly declined in popularity between 1910 and 1940, so well combines exterior distinctiveness with interior charm that it is following Victorian and Queen Anne in returning to fashion.

The big "sleeper" in Retro-homes, the market no one has yet caught on to, are the houses built in the 1950s. While houses of many styles were built during those years, including some very fine Colonial homes, the house that best represents the era of rock and roll, bobby socks and big American cars is the ranch-style. Often "split level" — the latest thing in 1955 — ranch-style homes exemplify the expansiveness, confidence and prosperity of their time. Low, open and broad, they offer large rooms adaptable to a variety of purposes. They typically have basement "rec rooms," where kids play and adults party, patios to symbolize the indoor-outdoor nature of the ranch life (even in the north and east), and big garages where that '57 Chevy BelAir can be seen by all the neighbors. Not only are these houses often good buys, their neighborhoods, now entering their seventies, are at the ideal age: well developed, with sidewalks, established landscaping including big trees, and nearby services. They offer a wonderful "start" for young people, affordable yet very Retro, recalling an era most Americans find far preferable to the time we face now.

NEW HOMES

Some people who want a Retroculture lifestyle also want a new house. New houses usually have fewer problems than old, need less in the way of repairs, and offer a chance to "personalize" a home.

Increasingly, you can find new homes built to reflect Retro styles. New colonial houses are readily available in most areas (though again, be wary of the real estate agent's definition of "colonial.") Recently, some builders have started constructing houses and even whole developments with a Victorian or Queen Anne flavor. These new houses have many of the desirable features of the originals, such as front porches, a variety of special-purpose rooms, and decorative woodwork and stained glass. When built as part of well-planned communities, they can offer the feel of a Victorian small town, with all the neighborliness, security and sense of community those towns had.

Another way to get a "new old" house is to have it special built. Plans for a wide variety of styles are readily found. Blueprints for well-designed, largely authentic colonial homes have been widely available, often through home or architecture magazines, since the 1930s. Recently, magazines such as *Victoria* have advertised house plans for Victorian and Queen Anne houses. If your taste runs to the Early American, you may find one of the many kits for log homes of interest; these are relatively inexpensive, a good choice for a first house or a second home in the country, and offer the feel of the log cabin that played a central role in our nation's settlement.

An imaginative way to build your own Retro-home is to find an older house you like, then duplicate it in your own setting. Of course, this requires the cooperation of the current owners, but many people would be flattered to be asked. An architect can easily make the plans from the original house. This approach offers the option of duplicating a house your own family used to live in. Perhaps you have fond memories of your grandparents' bungalow, or a fine Queen Anne where your great aunts lived, a place you used to love visiting in the summer as a child. You always wished you could somehow go back there, but the setting is inappropriate, or the neighborhood has deteriorated, or it is too far away from where you work. Well then, recreate it! Have the blueprints made from the original house, and build it where you want it. Now you have the best of both worlds: a brand-new house, where you want it, that brings with it all those treasured family memories — Retroculture at its finest!

Most Americans want to own a house. But economic realities being what they are, many of us must put that desire off for a while, and live for now in an apartment or a condominium. From a Retroculture standpoint, this need not be too great a sacrifice. You can find Retro condos and apartments in most parts of the country.

The best of these are, of course, in older buildings. Many cities have elegant apartment buildings constructed in the late 19th or early 20th centuries. After all, Fifth Avenue in New York, one of the nation's most desirable addresses — then and now — is all apartments and condos, many built before World War II. They offer Retro living at its most elegant, equal to anything a private house can provide.

In many cities, these once highly fashionable apartment buildings are in areas close to the city center, areas now not fashionable but consequently affordable. You may be able to afford condo or apartment Retro-living much more cheaply than you think, especially if you are willing to be an urban pioneer. Further, many of these areas are now coming back, with the middle class moving back into them as it discovers the advantages of living close to town. Young single people and couples often find the merit of living close by the city's many cultural attractions quite desirable, and they are resurrecting these buildings and neighborhoods. A tour of the city where you want to live can show you some of these areas and reveal just how nicely some apartment-dwellers in earlier times lived.

Some people may still think that to have a Retro-home, you have to be rich, or least well off. It's just not true. Of course, if you want a genuine Colonial on Boston's Beacon Hill, or a Victorian on San Francisco's Russian Hill, you are going to need a pretty good income. But there are lots of opportunities to find Retro-homes that are relatively inexpensive.

Remember that in the past, people did not expect as much space as some modern people think they need. Parents shared a bedroom, children usually did the same, and the kids' bedroom was also their playroom. One all-purpose living room was sufficient, without separate rec rooms, family rooms, and the like, at least in middle class homes. Upscale houses had more, smaller rooms, which makes them good for growing families today, but most did not have the huge expanses of space that became fashionable in the last forty years. Usually, a house had just one bathroom. Because people had better manners — something Retro people also cultivate — it was possible to live closer together without getting in each other's way.

What sufficed in terms of space for our parents and grandparents can be sufficient for us also, at least when we are starting out. Nor need we regard a small house as a hardship. Shared space, instead of everyone having "his own space," helps individual lives come together in a genuine family. It teaches consideration for others, punctuality, efficient use of time, quietness, and self-discipline, among the virtues our ancestors prized. The home is the first and most important school, and a small house is the best school of good manners.

Of course, as the family grows and your income rises, you may both want and need more space. But by starting small, you may also be able to start early in your quest for your very own Retro-home.

"TURNING BACK THE CLOCK" WITH THE HOME YOU HAVE

Retroculture need not start with finding a new home; it can begin with the house you have, if you have one. Depending on the age and style of your house, you may be able to make it into a fine Retro-home — and have some fun in the process.

The first step in taking your own house Retro is to determine just what is possible. Obviously, this includes such things as budget, your ability to put up with the temporary mess of reconstruction, and your house's setting. If going Retro with your own home means it will no longer fit in the neighborhood, that is a constraint you will want to respect.

Less obvious but perhaps most important is the question of what you can do with your house without violating its architectural integrity. Few if any Retroculture people would take, for example, a Queen Anne house and modernize it with picture windows, aluminum siding, dropped ceilings, and removal of all the wonderful turned decorative woodwork, filigree, and stained glass. We would recognize that as a hideous violation of the house's architectural integrity, the result

FIGURE 2. The Carson Mansion in Eureka, Northern California. (Source: Cory Maylett, Wikimedia Commons)

of which would be neither a modern house nor a Queen Anne but a mockery of the first and a desecration of the second.

But the same constraint works the other way. You will have difficulty taking a house built to a modern style and "antiquing" it without violating its integrity and creating, not a Retro-home, but a hopeless and tasteless mishmash. You cannot make a ranch-style home into a Victorian, nor into a colonial (though some builders have tried the latter, with unhappy results). The addition to a home, which is built to look modern, of "cutsie" fake bay windows, New Orleans-style iron grille columns, Victorian stained glass and country-house shutters will not create a Retro feel, but its opposite: an overwhelming sensation of bad taste. If the owner went on and added white-painted tractor tires by the driveway, a busted sofa on the front porch and several automobiles up on jacks and refrigerators without doors scattered about the yard, such a house could easily be mistaken for the local West Virginia consulate.

The point at which to begin determining what is possible with your house is, then, asking yourself, "What have I got to work with?" What is the basic style of your house? When was it built, and what historic period does it represent? What can be done that is consistent with its architecture, and what would violate its architectural integrity? You may know enough about your house and about architecture generally to answer these questions yourself. If not, you may answer them after some research in your local library, or you may prefer to ask an architect, an historian, or a friend or neighbor knowledgeable in this area to help you.

In general, especially with older homes, the safest way to take your house Retro is restoration: taking it back to what it was like when it was built. With Colonial, Victorian, Queen Anne, and inter-war styles, this is most often what you will want to do. It is safe, because it restores the house's integrity rather than threatening it. The results are usually pleasing, because you are most often removing what doesn't belong and replacing it with what does (the original design was usually a good one). It is Retro, because when you are done, you will have a home that looks and feels like an earlier era, the time when it was built.

Here again, you will have to determine just what is possible. If, for example, you have a genuine Colonial house, you probably won't want to get rid of indoor plumbing, central heating, electricity or a kitchen equipped with a range and refrigerator. Pure restoration won't be practical. If you have a big Victorian house, you may want more than the original single bathroom, and you probably won't need the servants' quarters for servants; you will want to use those rooms for other purposes. If, however, you have a bungalow from the 1920s, it may be possible to restore it to its original state, with only such minor, almost invisible changes as air conditioning and a place for the refrigerator in the kitchen (ice boxes usually went in an enclosed entryway or on a porch).

The key to restoration is careful research. Before you begin, you will want to determine just how your house did look, inside and out, when it was built. This can be easy or very difficult, depending on the house's age and how much it was rebuilt over the years. You may do it yourself, by seeking the original blueprints, talking to people who lived in the house when it was new, or learning how to read "clues" that signal moved walls, changed entryways and porches, bricked-over windows and the like. Or, you may want to get an architect or professional restorer to do that work for you. Whichever route you take, do it right: there is nothing so unfortunate as putting a lot of money into restoration only to find out you got it wrong. Even if your goal is not a pure restoration, you will want to make changes on the basis of knowledge: of knowing how it was originally, so you realize just what you are changing and whether what you plan is appropriate.

This part of restoration (not the dust and disorder of rebuilding) can be fun. In doing your research, you will learn a great deal about your home, the people who lived in it and your neighborhood and community. That knowledge adds greatly to the pleasure of living in your Retro-home, because it anchors your life in the earlier time you are seeking to recapture.

But what if you do live in modern house? Does respect for its architectural integrity mean you cannot take it Retro? Not necessarily. Depending on the style of your new house, you may be able to "back date" it — so long as you do so in ways consistent with its style. For example, if you live in a new colonial-style house, you can safely make it more colonial, with changes ranging from the addition of hardwood, broad-board floors and small-paned windows through appropriate dormers, exterior and interior doors and shutters to a salt-box addition on the rear. Or, if you live in a new ranch-style house, you can probably take it back to the 1950s without creating an architectural mishmash. The key is to understand what your new house is modelled on — what historic style is reflects — and back date it to reflect that style more closely. Again, you may research for yourself what that might mean for your house, or get some professional assistance in doing so.

For both new houses and old, one of the easiest and least expensive ways to take your home Retro is with paint. Simply painting your house in colors that would have been used in the time its style represents — Williamsburg colors for a colonial, or the bright Victorian colors we see on San Francisco's famous "painted ladies," or white with dark green trim on a home from the 1920s — can make a big difference in its Retro-look.

Similarly, changing the landscaping can be relatively easy and inexpensive, yet make a real difference in whether your house looks "period." If, for example, you have a colonial house, you can make it look much more like an actual 18th-century home by planting a colonial herb garden/kitchen garden, or perhaps by making the back or side yard into the sort of formal garden 18th-century people liked, a miniature Versailles with formal beds and hedgerows, even some boxwoods (if you're patient), a maze or some espaliered fruit trees. For the Victorian look, a rose garden is perfect, perhaps with a gazebo if you have the space. Heritage plants, both flowers and vegetables, are now widely available even from major seed companies like Burpee's and Park's. Batchelor's buttons, cosmos, pansies, and that staple of the Victorians, *viola odorata*, the powerfully scented violets children sold on the street corners, can surround your home with the colors and fragrances of the 19th century. If you own a 1950s ranch-style, your pride will show in your perfectly cut, edged, and trimmed, absolutely weedless bluegrass lawn.

Whether you choose to remodel extensively or merely paint and landscape, there is probably a long list of actions you can take to make your present house look Retro — if it was designed from the outset to reflect an earlier period, and if that period is the one you seek to recreate. If it is just a generic modern house, with no aspirations to reflect a past style, or if it is, say, colonial when your interest is Victorian, then your options are more limited (assuming bad taste is not one of them). But even in these cases, your situation is not hopeless. We have been talking about how your house looks from the outside. Now, let's look inside.

RETRO-INTERIORS

There is nothing new about the idea of decorating a home in the style of an earlier time. At least from the late 19th-century Arts & Crafts Movement onward, interior furnishings have often hearkened back to earlier styles. The most popular and enduring has been colonial.

What is new is the range of periods for which furnishings are readily available. Until just a few years ago, colonial was about all that was available in reproductions. If you wanted Victorian, or Craftsman, or Art Deco, you had to dig around for antiques (and pay the price). When it came to finding wallpapers, appropriate paint colors, fabrics and so on, you were in trouble.

No more. Now, there is a vast selection. Retroculture has caught on in interior decorating, to the point where you can find reproductions of almost everything you need for most common earlier styles. Victorian you will find in lush abundance; Washington, D.C., has a shop devoted solely to Mission-style reproductions; your local hardware supplier offers Art Deco bathroom mirrors, light fixtures, and pedestal sinks. The pages of almost any magazine on home furnishing present wallpapers, tiles, and fabrics from Victorian through the 1950s. *Victoria* magazine carries ads for even the most obscure necessities for late 19th- and early 20th-century living, e.g., a shop specializing in Victorian silk lampshades ("Shades of the Past").

There are, however, some ways to be Retro in furnishing your home that go beyond what the average person might consider. They reflect the desire of Retro-people to capture as much as possible of the feel of life in the past, to create in their home a warm, comfortable cocoon made of memories, of family, and of those who may have lived in that same house in times gone by.

One way to do this is to decorate your house around family memories. You can try to recapture the feel of specific places and people you remember fondly. If you're lucky, you may have some or many family heirlooms you can feature in your own home. You may even have enough to make a room or rooms into duplicates of rooms you remember in the house where you grew up, or that of a favorite aunt or grandparent.

What if you are not among the lucky ones with heirlooms? The range of reproductions now available, plus what you may find in the antique stores and the flea markets, can provide you with "instant heirlooms": pieces that closely or exactly duplicate furniture, wallpaper patterns, carpets or pictures from homes you remember. Nothing is quite so rewarding as suddenly spotting the same kind of chair your grandfather used to sit in, or the type of lamp that hung in the front hall, or the Mail Pouch Tobacco ad that stood above your grandfather's desk in his store. You have found again what seemed lost forever — which is what Retroculture is all about.

Here as elsewhere, there are ways to get started that fit almost any budget. Antiques are too expensive? Then look for reproductions. Reproductions also cost too much? Hunt in the flea markets, garage sales, estate auctions and junk shops. Just as with houses, some periods are less expensive than others. If Victorian is too pricey, or Colonial, begin with the styles of the 1930s, 40s, and 50s. Too young to be real antiques, these "collectibles" can often be found very reasonably — more reasonably that the cheap but pricey junk, made more often than not of sawdust or pasteboard, that fills the modern furniture stores.

You can also get a leg up on Retroculture while keeping costs down by going Retro in some areas most people don't think of. One such area is appliances. Nothing gives a home that Retro feeling so much as a kitchen with the classic old-fashioned stove, standing up high on legs, the oven set above and beside the burners which in turn have a shield behind them and a shelf (handy for warming plates) above them. If they are gas they almost never break. The local used appliance place may have a nice selection of old refrigerators; those from the 1930s and 40s were beautifully made and run without a murmur for many decades, though of course you do have to defrost them. Around your Retro kitchen, you can scatter a side-opener toaster, an old electric mixer, maybe a breadbox rescued from the family attic or picked up for a few dollars at a garage sale. Don't be afraid of an appliance just because it is old; remember, old also means simpler, sturdier, and much easier to fix if it does need some repair. Go by condition when you buy, not age, and you will be surprised at what you can find that will provide years of dependable service. You will also be surprised at how convenient many old appliances are to use: side-opener toasters are perfect for bagels.

Whether in your kitchen or elsewhere, don't worry if your Retro-home's furnishings have a few modern anachronisms. Unless you are very lucky, you probably won't find a good old-fashioned dishwasher, because there were so few of them. So, get a modern one; just put panels on it that blend with the Retro-colors of your kitchen (cream or yellow with red trim was big in the 1920s), and it will hardly be noticed. Speakers for your stereo? Put them in a discreet corner, with perhaps an Art Nouveau lamp on a table near them to draw the observer's attention to itself. Window air conditioners? Again, get a color that blends with the walls and curtains, and don't worry about them. People coming into your home will have so much else to look at that they will never see them, and you will be so accustomed to them that you won't either. Remember, it's the overall effect that counts, and a few unavoidable anachronisms won't detract from that if you've gone Retro with everything else.

In the Retro-home, the goal is to recapture the feel of an earlier time, not create a picture for a magazine ad. Those earlier homes were lived in, not just put on display. As you make your home Retro, think less of museums and more of your grandmother's house. Grandma or Nana probably had many things that weren't new and perfect, that showed the use and wear of ordinary life. She bought her furniture and knick-knacks and mugs over a period of many years, and they reflected a mixture of styles. She had some items that may not have been in the most fashionable taste, but she liked them and they said something about her. Let your own Retro-home be likewise. Make it so that it is comfortable for you. Don't worry too much about mixing eras; in the old days, almost everybody did.

RETRO-NEIGHBORHOODS

The doorway to the Retro-home is, ideally, a time-lock; once you are through it, you are in another era. But wouldn't it be nice if that time-lock could be positioned a bit further out, at the entrance to the neighborhood? Depending on where you live or are looking to live, it can be.

If you are not already settled but are looking for a home, your search may turn up a Retro-neighborhood in a variety of places. The most promising is simply an old town. Some towns feel remarkably untouched by the withering hand of time; put the people on the street back in straw boaters or long skirts and convert the Nissans into Tin Lizzies and presto! you're back in 1925. The Northeast, the Mid-Atlantic region and the Midwest are rich in such towns; in the West, they are somewhat more rare and likely to be expensive. They are expensive because towns offer what many people want; a sense of community, a place that is friendly to the pedestrian, not just the automobile, and buildings that serve a variety of purposes — stores, offices, and houses — but all work comfortably together.

If you can't find a whole Retro-town, you may find a Retro-neighborhood within a town, a city, or even a suburb. Often built in the Victorian era — every town had its "rich row" of great Victorian houses, where the local *grands fromages* made their residences — or between the wars, these neighborhoods, like old towns, retain their characters. Good luck or that great preserver, poverty, has kept the schlockers at bay, and it takes little imagination to see them as they were when they were built. In fact, they may be even nicer now, because the trees have had a chance to grow big. Today, many residents of such neighborhoods are waking up the value of what they have and are taking measures to preserve it by zoning, designating local historic districts, and forming volunteer compacts among the neighbors. Such activities add further to the old-fashioned nature of the neighborhood by turning it into a genuine community where people know each other and share a common interest and purpose.

The key to finding a Retro-neighborhood is time. If you have to move from Tucson to Cleveland in a hurry and have two weeks to find a house, your chances of discovering a Retro-neighborhood are not that great. Unless you already know a great deal about Cleveland or can find a real estate agent who understands Retroculture, you are likely to end up in another dreary housing tract. But if you have time to search around a bit, you will find such Retro-delights as Medina, the Victorian town mentioned in Chapter I; Hudson, a town seemingly transplanted from early 19th-century New England; and the part of Lakewood nearest Lake Erie, a surprisingly affordable neighborhood of magnificent homes built between 1900 and 1940.

It may be wise, if inconvenient in the short run, to move into temporary quarters for a while and look around for what you really want—not just your dream Retro-home, but a Retro-neighborhood as well. Get to know the nooks and crannies of your new city; they will almost certainly offer some pleasant surprises. Not only will you end up settling in to what you really want, you may well save a good deal of cash in the bargain. That house and neighborhood the real estate agent swears can't be had for less than $200,000 may be available for a fraction of that price, once you know where to look.

What if you are already settled? What can you do with the neighborhood you have?

That depends on what it offers you to work with. If your house is in an older community, you will have at hand the raw material for a Retro-neighborhood. Just ask yourself, what was this neighborhood like when it was in its prime? Quickly, in your mind's eye you will see how the houses looked before the porches were stripped off and the picture windows went in, and how your street appeared when the tree lawn held big shade trees and the cars were parked in the alley. Your task, as a pioneer in Retroculture, is to bring your neighbors around to share that same vision and join together in bringing it to life.

One of the signs that Retroculture is taking hold on the American imagination is a growing movement to build new old-fashioned towns. Nothing offers more hope for our collective future, in terms of the place we would like to live. These new towns offer more than just houses built to historic patterns. They offer the integration of houses, open spaces, streets (designed very much with pedestrians in mind),[6] stores, and places of employment. In these new old towns, you can often walk to the store or even to work, come home for lunch, stop and talk with neighbors sitting out on their front porch, and in general live in ways not too different from those your grandparents knew and enjoyed. Here, the best of the old and the new are combined, which is just what Retroculture seeks.

The leaders of this "New Urbanism" movement are the dynamic husband-and-wife duo we met in our first chapter, architects Andres Duany and Elizabeth Plater-Zyberk, the creators of Seaside, Florida. They argued their case that "the future does not have to be imagined so much as remembered" in a notable article in *The Wilson Quarterly* "The Second Coming of the American Small Town." They note that:

> All of the elements of towns already exist in the modern American suburb. For various historical reasons, though, they have been improperly assembled, artificially separated into 'pods' strung along 'collector roads' intended to speed the flow of traffic... These elements are the makings of a great cuisine, but they have never been properly combined. It is as if we were expected to eat, rather than a completed omelet, first the eggs, then

---

[6] One sees an echo of this via the "pedestrianization schemes" that are being implemented across many European cities. — Editor.

the cheese, and then the green peppers... We believe, quite simply, that all of these elements should once again be assembled into traditional towns.

For the current unhappy state of affairs, the authors point the finger of blame at local codes and the planners and traffic engineers who write them:

> In every community, the code is a kind of constitution that lays out the rules that will order the life of the city, the rules that describe the form of urbanism that will emerge, just as the American Constitution contains within it the lineaments of American society. ... [I]n most American communities, it is quite easy to conclude that the single most important constitutional principle is that cars must be happy.

In pointing to the codes as the problem, Duany and Plater-Zyberk also point to a solution: the re-writing of those codes. Since Seaside, Duany and Plater-Zyberk have designed some forty new old towns, some of which have been built, including Tannin, Alabama, Nance Canyon, California, and Kentlands, Maryland, near Washington, D.C. If you are moving to a new area, you might want to see if one of their towns has been built where you are moving.

RETRO-HOMES IN RETROSPECT

Taking your house Retro is a good starting point for your Retroculture life. It is not difficult, it need not be expensive if you use your imagination (and local junk shops and yard sales), and it can be immensely rewarding. As you create a "nest" that offers the memories, sense of place and feel of the time you love, you give yourself an ever-present vacation from the troubles of the present. When you come home at night and take off your coat, you leave the stress of the job and the commute far behind, farther than mere geography allows, for you enter a different and gentler era. As Retroculture catches on more widely, you may be able to push the time boundary outward still more, to the doorway of your neighborhood. It is a pleasant prospect, and for those who have already done it, a source of unceasing refreshment.

Perhaps most important, the Retro-home is the place where the Retro-family gathers, lives and grows. To that family, the center of the Retroculture life, let us now turn.

FIGURE 3. *American Homes and Gardens*, p. 72. (New York: Munn and Co, 1905)

CHAPTER V

∽

Retro-Families

People seeking a Retroculture lifestyle usually want to surround themselves with things that remind them of the way life used to be. But Retroculture, at its heart, is not about things. Rather, it is about the quality of life that Americans used to enjoy. Quality of life may and often does express itself in things, but things do not of themselves create a desirable quality of life. If you ask yourself what made your grandparents' lives better than the life we live now, your answer probably is not their home or their furniture or the entertainment they enjoyed, though these all may have been better than what we have now. At the heart of the matter, rather, lie intangible qualities like community, security, stability, contentment, togetherness, and love. And at the center of these lies the family.

We need not go on here about the sad state into which the family has fallen in our own day. The statistics about broken homes, children born to single parents, and similar signs of family breakdown are familiar to any newspaper reader. Rather, our purpose here is to talk about how to build families up again.

Americans instinctively know that a strong family is good. They also know that in the past, we had strong, healthy families. In a national survey, 70% of those polled said that family and community life was better in the past than it is today; only 15% thought it was worse.

Retroculture suggests that since we want strong families, and we know family life was better in the past than it is today, it is obvious what we need to do: rediscover and recover the qualities that made families strong back then. Of course, as in most other areas, we will not recreate the past exactly. Some things have changed beyond our control. But by looking at family life in the past, we can learn "new old" ways to make our families stronger under today's conditions. We can move into the future armed with the lessons of the past, instead of having to learn those lessons over again the hard way.

What made families strong in the past? Perhaps the best way to answer that question is simply to think about your grandparents. How did they regard and treat each other? What kinds of things did they do together? How did they get through the crises that have beset families in every time? (The Great Depression of the 1930s was, after all, no picnic.)

As in much of Retroculture, family memories are often the best place to start in recapturing what we want from the past. Nor must the memories all be happy ones: then as now, families had difficulties brought on by their own mistakes and by the bad behavior of individual family members. From these too we can learn, as we watch, for example, how some members of the family made sacrifices to keep the whole family going in the face of the failures and weaknesses of others.

We can also learn a great deal about how families kept themselves strong in earlier times from books. Much of the literature from our nation's history revolves around family life, because it was so central; it was much more important than what governments or schools or even churches did. Novels and stories from the pre-war years, and especially from the 19th century, offer a vivid and compelling picture of family life. So do popular magazines of the time. See if your local library has issues of *The Saturday Evening Post*, *Colliers*, or *Life* magazine from the 1950s; you will find in their stories a great deal about families.

(Their ads, pictures, and news stories about the latest products also make them fun reading for anyone interested in Retroculture.)

From your own family memories and your reading, you may find it helpful to identify some of the things families used to do, actions than made them strong. These might include:

- **Really sharing their lives.** In the past, the family was not just an economic but also an emotional unit. Problems, frustrations, unhappiness were shared and thus lessened, just as successes and joys were shared and thus increased. The family, not the school counselor or the psychotherapist, was the place people first turned when things went wrong (or right). When dad got an unexpected raise, he rushed home, gathered up the family and took them all out to dinner to celebrate. When junior was having trouble in school, the whole family got involved to help, tutoring him, meeting with his teachers and the principal, and helping him discipline himself to study. When mom was overwhelmed with housework, everyone pitched in to share the load. What we now regard as individual crises or triumphs became family crises or triumphs, and through this sharing, the family grew strong.

- **Families spent a lot of time together.** They gathered every evening for family dinner, and usually for family breakfast as well. In the evenings, in the 1890s or 1920s, they sat together on the front porch, perhaps with some of the children playing nearby in the yard or the street. In the 1930s they gathered around the radio. And in the 1950s the whole family sat down together after dinner to watch *Gunsmoke* or the *The Ed Sullivan Show*. The home was not just a place where people slept, grabbed something to eat, or dropped their books as they came from school and headed straight for the mall. It was a place where people really lived together, spent time together, talked together.

- **Family activities,** and often family life at home as well, involved more than mom, dad, and the kids. Almost as important were grandparents, aunts, uncles and cousins. Holidays and birthdays were events for the extended family to celebrate together, as of course were such special times as weddings. There was lots of visiting back and forth; remember how grandma and grandpa always came to your house Christmas Eve, then went to your cousins for Christmas Day, making the regular rounds year by year? Vacations often revolved around visits to aunts and uncles, especially those who still lived in the country if you were in town. These activities kept people in touch closely enough that they really knew each other as individuals, not just as names on cards or letters. Grandparents, uncles, and aunts could and did play important roles in family crises. When mother got sick, the family sent to Pennsylvania for Aunt Lula, the family saint (most families back then had at least one) who always came and knew just what to do. If one of the children was having a rough time at home, he or she went off to visit the aunts for some release and recuperation. If in tough economic times mom and dad both had to work, grandma, not some stranger in a day care center, took care of the children. Especially through grandparents and great aunts and uncles, children developed an important sense of who their family was over the generations — and knew what kinds of things just "weren't done" in their family. This was a useful anchor and helpful guide in the difficult times of adolescence and early adulthood.

- **The family was the primary school.** It was understood that a child's learning, manners and morals reflected on his family, and the family, not the public school system, was every child's first and most important school. Schooling was done in many ways. Lots of homes, not just those of the wealthy, had good libraries of serious books. The noted author Russell Kirk speaks of how his

CHAPTER V. RETRO-FAMILIES

grandfather, the owner of a small restaurant in a Michigan railroad town, introduced him to good reading as a young boy in the 1920s:

> Frank Pierce was the only member of his family ever to have attended a liberal-arts college — and that for a few months, to study music. But he was a wise man, self-educated: his bookcases were crammed with sets of Dickens, Mark Twain, Hugo. He was well read in history, Macaulay particularly. Ridpath's four-volume *Encyclopedia of Universal History*, bound in calf, profusely illustrated, became Russell's introduction to historical consciousness. Presently his grandfather gave him a copy of van Loon's *Story of Mankind*, and later H.G. Well's *Outline of History*: Russell would come to sense that the latter, though so interesting, was quite wrong-headed.

Morals and manners were both subjects for early and careful education. Children were expected to learn how to behave at the dinner table, in company with adults, and in public at an early age: the spoiled, demanding, obnoxious child was not considered "cute" in those days. Moral instruction was woven into bedtime stories, and was also part of basic family life: children learned early how to share, to consider the needs of others (remember, most houses had only one bathroom), and to be responsible. Regular chores were an early part of family life, and the young boy's paper route or other job brought welcome income for the whole family; the money thus earned was not just his. Much of the literature about child-raising from the Victorian era through the inter-war years emphasized the need for the home to be the place where children learn the basics of successful life: self-discipline, modesty, hard work, saving, and the ability to sacrifice present pleasures for future needs. The home was the school of good citizenship.

From your own memories, you will undoubtedly be able to add to this list. And it may well be that your family still does many of these traditional things. But as you reflect on what families used to do, the ways they grew strong as families, you may come to realize how much we have lost. The television — the Devil's babysitter — the computer and cellphone, and pressure from the modern world to grow up too quickly have undermined family life, drawing children away from their families long before they are ready to make sound decisions on their own.

Suppose you want to go Retro in your family life, to rediscover some of the ways families used to live and thus recover the strength they used to have. Where can you begin?

The easiest place is with some of the activities families used to do together. Family dinner is a good place to start. With some planning, it is not impossible to arrange everyone's schedule so that, at a certain hour, they are home together for dinner. Allow enough time so everyone can pitch in and help make dinner, especially if mom works, and so that dinner is not just a "pit stop" but an hour out of the day for everyone to catch up on what others are doing. You'll be surprised how much more the day's events mean when you have a regular chance to share them with the rest of the family in dinner-table conversation. Problems that seemed overwhelming when you faced them alone become much more manageable once you've shared them with the rest of the family and gotten their advice and help.

Another good starting place is family activities. Take the whole family to the beach or the show or on a picnic. Doing things together that are fun for all allows everyone to relax with each other. Tensions in the home tend to disappear. Make family activities a regular event, and watch how the children begin to think in terms of the family's life instead of just their own lives.

It is usually up to parents to take the lead in sharing problems and hardships. But once the kids hear mom and dad doing it, they will become comfortable with it also. Too often, children nowadays seem to fear bringing problems to their parents, and it shouldn't be that way. A supportive, caring family makes the very real problems of growing up much more bearable. And mom and dad, in turn, can often find the children willing and able to pitch in and help when they are under too much stress from the job or the growing mountain of bills. Sharing difficulties builds strong families at least as much as sharing pleasures.

In fact, the notion of sharing burdens was fundamental in old-fashioned families. It's still a good idea. Right from the time they were toddlers, kids used to have chores. Maybe it was nothing more than slicing the bread before dinner, but the child still came to understand early that a family is a joint enterprise. Children respond well to this, because it gives them importance in their own eyes. As they grow, they take on ever-greater responsibilities — and learn personal responsibility in the process. Because their family is something in which they have a personal investment, it means more to them. And because it is a place where their labor and voice are needed and respected, they do not have to "find themselves" among their peers.

These are all Retro things families can do to begin coming together again. But Retroculture offers more than that. It is itself something families can do together. Taking your home and your family life Retro can be a shared enterprise.

Kids like to be on the cutting edge of fashion, and in the 21st century, that's Retroculture. They can and will take pleasure in being the first on their block to go Retro. There are lots of ways you can involve them. Some kids may share their parents' interest in taking the house Retro. If one of the children is approaching driving age and you are looking for a car, get a Retro "project car" and make its restoration a family project (an air-cooled VW Beetle is a good choice, or perhaps something from the 1950s; if you look in the "Antiques and Classics" column of your local paper's classified ads, you will find some cars from the 50s can be bought inexpensively).

The key to making Retroculture a shared family activity is to let each person take the lead in what he or she is most interested in. Perhaps a son is interested in architecture: let him research the architectural history of the house and take the lead in determining what is needed to restore it. Or maybe a daughter is interested in clothes and sewing: let her be in charge of taking the family's sense of clothing style Retro. If mom's interest is local history, she can anchor the house and the family's life in "how the town used to be." If each member of the family can be the leader in his or her particular favorite part of Retroculture, each comes to depend on the other while at the same time being the "recognized authority" in his or her own special field. For children, an opportunity to serve as a leader in the family is especially important; it is another example of the family's role as the prime educator.

Two areas of study are especially helpful and interesting in enabling a family to go Retro. The first, which we have touched on, is local history. If you live in an older community, your neighborhood and town have a history all their own. The more you learn of it, the more interesting your local life will be. Why was your community founded, and what was its original role for the people who lived there? Why has it developed as it has? What was that old house down at the crossroads — an inn, perhaps, with a turnpike tollhouse across from it where you can still find remains of a foundation? Where did the interurban electric trolley line run, and how did it change your town when it arrived in the 1890s? Just learning what your town, neighborhood and street looked like in various times past can make your present life there more meaningful. Perhaps your community already has a local historical society, maybe with a small museum; if so, joining it is an excellent way to learn about "your" history. If not, why not start one?

Similarly, a great way to get in touch with your past is family history. You might start with genealogy: who were your ancestors, where did they come from and what did they do? Oral history is also useful here: ask your older family members to recall their childhoods, their parents and grandparents, aunts and uncles, and record their answers for future generations. The furniture and other heirlooms you may possess all have their histories: find out who owned them and see what their stories are. Some of the houses your family used to live in may still be standing; go see them, and take the kids. Often, the people who live there now are happy to let you tour the house and share your knowledge and memories of it with them.

Discovering your family's own history makes Retroculture personal. Your children will find the Victorian era all the more interesting when they look at it through the lens of their great or great-great-grandparents' lives. As those ancestors become real to them through family history, they will knit the family together across time. The way those earlier members of your family lived, their values, beliefs, religious faith, hard work, and even eccentricities, all offer useful lessons and often models for the Retro-family today. They provide a stabilizing influence, one that can contest against the message of instant gratification preached by social media and today's materialist culture.

Recovering the past in your family's life is the heart of Retroculture for the family. These ideas offer some ways to help start that process. Now, let's take a look at some of the specific ideas the past suggests about the things families do: about life in a Retroculture family.

STARTING A RETROCULTURE FAMILY: DATING

Many young people who are dating do not seem to think of it in terms of starting a family. Since the "sexual revolution" of the 1960s, dating has looked, not toward the future family, but to immediate gratification: sex. Dating has become a game of conquest, "hooking up," with a "successful" date (at least from the male's perspective) being one where the couple "went all the way." The result has been an attack on men and the sad degradation (especially of women) from the gentle art of courtship and wooing to something little different from animals in rut.

Retroculture people look at dating differently. In the past we seek to recapture, dating was part of an unhurried, innocent and entertaining process in which young people gradually got to know those of the opposite sex as people, and, in the process, grew in maturity and refinement into adults. They key to this process of growth and maturation was a simple but firm rule, of the sort our grandparents called "morals:" you don't "go all the way" on a date.

The old moral rule is even more important in our time. The nasty fact is, in the face of Sexually Transmitted Diseases (STDs), there is no such thing as "safe sex" outside marriage. The various devices that supposedly promise safety don't: they fail much too often. The only real safety lies in returning to the old rule against casual sex.

To Retroculture people, STDs are a frightening argument against "free love," as our forefathers called it, but by no means the only argument. As the sad wreckage around us argues plaintively, casual sex, sex outside a long-term, loving relationship sanctified by marriage, leads not to happiness but to lonely, self-centered misery. The children of the sexual revolution, those who came to see sex as the purpose of a relationship, are now finding themselves in a dreary old age, the victims of failed marriages and unhappy liaisons. They never went through the process of growth and maturation dating used to bring: it all happened too fast. The "triumphs" of sexual conquest they celebrated as college students left them unable to see the opposite sex as people, only as objects. With no commitment to marriage as an institution, it too became a temporary arrangement, leaving only divorce and loneliness in its wake. Not for them the stable, contented later life they saw their grandparents live: the bright fire of desire easily requited has left only ashes.

Those old-fashioned morals our grandparents believed in reflected what men and women had learned about themselves and each other over countless generations. Retroculture seeks to recapture that wisdom and its fruits of enduring, emotionally satisfying relationships, by starting right. Dating, in Retroculture life, is not about "quickie" sex. It is about getting to know people of the opposite sex as people. That takes time and experience. It takes the kinds of innocent entertainments our parents and their parents enjoyed: dances and parties (chaperoned), picnics and Sunday-school outings, going to dinner at the boyfriend's or girlfriend's house, (family involvement, not family exclusion, should be the rule), rides in the country and days on a sailboat. It also takes rules, firmly enforced: Retro-people do not allow "sleeping over," and if a young lady comes home late, she can expect momma and poppa waiting at the door for an explanation.

If, by returning to the old rules and the old ways, we can give young people today some time, if we can take some of the pressure off them, they can grow and mature just as their forebears did. As they do so, as they learn to understand other people in ways more than skin-deep, they too will be able to find someone who can mean much more to them than a one-night stand. They too can experience that magic moment when they realize, "This is someone with whom I would like to spend the rest of my life."

MARRYING

In the past, marriage was usually the most important voluntary event in a person's life. Why? Because life forever after was irrevocably different. Just as with the involuntary events of birth and death, there was no going back; marriage was indeed "'til death do us part." Divorce was legally difficult and also a great scandal; a divorced person was simply "not received" in good society.

Now, of course, divorce is legally easy in most places and seldom carries a social stigma. But that need not keep Retroculture people from sharing our ancestors' deep commitment to the institution of marriage. Like them, we may regard marriage as a lifetime commitment, something entered into carefully and solemnly, and, once done, done for life. A number of modern studies of marriage have all come to the same conclusion: marriages succeed when both the husband and the wife have a strong commitment, not only to each other, but to the institution of marriage as well.

A personal resolution to regard marriage as sacred and indissoluble, as all society regarded it in our great-grandparents' day, leads us to see wisdom in another of their practices: long engagements. To select wisely in choosing a partner for life, you need to know the party in question very, very well. That takes time, time offered by a long engagement. Here as elsewhere, modern society emphasizes speed, pressure, and getting it done. Retroculture, looking to the past, counsels patience, restraint, and taking the long view. By the time you reach your Golden Anniversary, those extra months or even years you put into getting to know each other before you married will look like a very good investment, one that has paid many happy dividends.

Part of the reason people used to have long engagements was to help them look beyond "being in love." Fiery passions burn bright, but as our ancestors were warned in many of the novels that used to be popular, they may also burn briefly. An enduring marriage is built on more than romantic passion; it takes shared interests, compatible personalities, a mutually agreeable division of duties, and all the other things that only time discovers. The Amish, those Ur-practitioners of Retroculture, have a saying, "Kissing fades, cooking don't." When was the last time you heard of an Amish divorce?

Most Retroculture people will want a church wedding. Nowadays, with many churches, you can pretty much just walk in and get married. In the old days, it wasn't quite like that. The church required that those who wanted to get married spend some time studying marriage and coming to understand the awesome commitment it entails. Churches had regular programs to prepare people for marriage, involving reading, discussions with the minister, and prayerful consideration of just what it was they were about to do. Some churches have kept this practice, or would be happy to revive it on request. It is something Retroculture people will want to consider. Like a long engagement, it is a small investment with potentially great returns. And it brings into the marriage from the outset someone who will later be needed to make it a happy and lasting one: God.

When, finally, after due and careful preparation, the great day of the wedding arrives, Retroculture says: do it right. Life's greatest moment deserves pulling out all the stops. Make it a great Victorian wedding, with a dress future generations will treasure, bridesmaids and flower girls, "The Wedding March" from *Tannhaüser*—the works.

After all, you're only going to do it once. Make it truly a day to remember. More than any other, it is the first day of the rest of your life.

Today as in the past, most married couples are going to want children. But when they come, the new family faces a question most families did not face in the recent past: should mom stay home with the kids or continue to work? The question is not an easy one. Economic and social pressures combine to keep mom at work, with the kids farmed out to day care.

But Retroculture has an important message here: you simply can't "do it all." Those countless past generations who understood that the kids needed mom at home were right. They reflected once again the wisdom of the ages, what people have learned about themselves over time. Children deprived of a mother's constant care too often grow up badly, and a mother who tries to be both an adequate mom and a career woman stretches herself beyond what mortal flesh can bear. Nature's law is writ in stone: dad is the provider, and mom is mom. The price of any other arrangement is usually high, for all concerned.

It may surprise some people to learn that this is not the first time we have faced a society and an economy that pressured mothers to join the work force. When the industrial revolution began in the late-18th century, whole families — children as well as mother and father — were often pressed by economic need to go into the factories. The Victorians, people of sound morals and high purpose, came to see that this was wrong. It wrecked families, destroyed childhood and fed widespread social problems. One of the most important social movements of the Victorian age was the crusade for a "family wage" — a wage adequate for the man of the house to support his family. By the latter part of the 19th century, the family wage was general, and the pattern we know from our own families' history was the norm: father went to work and the mother and children stayed home.

In recent decades, we have lost much of what the Victorians achieved (and not only the family wage). But the basic fact they understood remains true: kids need mom at home and, in turn, mom needs to be home with the kids. Just as they need her constant attention and instruction to grow into useful, productive citizens, she needs time to attend and instruct them, so as to be the mother she wants to be. So the matter comes down to this: how can we live as a family should on one income?

Fortunately, Retroculture also has an answer to this question, an answer from the past: make do with fewer things. Americans used to take pride in "making do," in having a good, solid family life even when there was little money. Everyone contributed to the effort to economize, and all the little efforts added up. A family can make do with a small house, as we noted in the last chapter. It can make do with one car in most cases, if pop will take public transportation to work (just like granddad took the streetcar). Clothes can be passed from one child to the next as they grow. Not every dinner must include expensive meat (and some meatless meals will help the family's health). One phone, one television (or perhaps better none with children in the house), are enough. Kids do not need smartphones or videogames. After all, most people lived like this until the great boom after World War II, and it doesn't seem to have hurt them. In fact, since "making do" was a shared family enterprise, it helped make families stronger and taught children responsibility. It can do the same today.

A Congregational minister, Charlie Luckey, used to say, "We are commanded to love people and use things, not the other way around." In the last few decades, too many people have come to love things. The family is the best place to start setting our priorities straight again. If we love people and use things, we will find that a family can get by with fewer things while providing the time for love, especially the love of a mother for her children. Far better for a family that there be only one car in the garage, and that perhaps an old one, but that mother be home with and for her children. Our grandparents managed that on less income than most of us, even in the straightened middle class, have today. By living with the same sense of economy and making do they had, we can too.

RETROCULTURE AND SCHOOL

As we have said before, from a Retroculture standpoint, the first and most important school for all children is their family. From the child's earliest months on, he or she is learning. In the past, parents were careful about what their young children learned. They saw to it that stories taught sound morals; that good conduct was rewarded and bad swiftly though fairly punished; and that manners were inculcated right from the outset. They were careful to exclude bad influences on their children — then other children with bad behavior, now more the television, internet, videogames and other degraded forms of "entertainment." At the same time, they labored to provide good influences: toys that encouraged creativity (remember Erector Sets and Lincoln Logs?),[7] helped establish gender identity (dollhouses for girls, toy trains for boys) and taught reasoning (games and puzzles); playmates whose families also taught good manners and morals; and, very importantly, the regular company of adults, not just other kids. Often, grandmothers, aunts, or even family friends became what we might now call "mentors" to young children, taking them along on adult activities like shopping or eating out, letting them help in the kitchen, and confronting them, lovingly, with expectations of adult-like behavior. The understanding was common in times past that children could play and have fun like children, yet at the same time demonstrate "grown up" behavior in the company of adults. As, indeed, they can.

Education in the family did not stop when the child began formal schooling. The family continued to encourage development of the mind, through such acts as subscribing to good magazines, buying good books, and taking family outings to places like the art museum and local historical sites. Equally, it continued to help form the child's character, through work that contributed to the family, attendance at

---

[7] These were both toy sets made from metal and wood respectively, with which one could construct various miniature buildings, forts etc. Both were invented between 1912 and 1920.

church and Sunday School, and an insistence on observing such values as honesty, self-sacrifice, and respect for elders within the family.

Retroculture families will want to consider doing these or similar kinds of things today. As Retroculture always reminds us, what worked then can work now. By seeing the family as the first and most important school, we can help our own children grow into the solid citizens we want them to be — and that our country needs, now more than ever.

But when we talk about education, we must also face an unhappy difference between our situation today and that our parents and grandparents faced. Then, when children reached school age, we could send them off to the public schools with confidence that the sound lessons and values they learned at home would be built upon by the school. Sadly, that is no longer true. Over the past fifty years, many public school systems have virtually collapsed. In 1960, the main problems in schools were talking in class and running in the hall; in the early 21st century, they may well be drugs, guns, and murder. Even in schools without outright crime, discipline has often broken down, effective teaching has been sacrificed to the latest educational theories, and students face the prospect of graduating without knowing how to read, reason, or do mathematics competently. If values are taught at all, they are not the solid, old values our grandparents learned from their McGuffy readers, but values like "diversity," that do little to teach children how to behave. Conduct and character are not considered to be part of a "modern" education.

What is a Retro parent to do? The answer is, look for a Retro school. Look for a school that teaches reading through phonics and math without calculators, that grades on conduct and character development, and that promptly expels students who disrupt school discipline. In other words, look for a good 1950s school.

Sometimes, you may have to move to a new school district. Or, you may be able to work with other parents to move your school board in the Retro direction. In some states, like Minnesota, you can send your child to whatever public school you choose, regardless of where you live. This "choice in education" policy is spreading; you might want to help it along in your state and city.

Another option is schools run by churches. Often, the most Retro schools are the local Catholic schools, and many parents who aren't Catholic or even religious send their children there because of the discipline, the dedicated teachers, and the solid, old-fashioned instruction. Protestant churches too sometimes have good schools attached to them. And some communities have private day or boarding schools not connected with churches that maintain the old standards. All these schools cost money, of course. But from a Retroculture standpoint, nothing is more important than your children's future. Do what many of our grandparents did, especially those who came to this country as poor immigrants: tighten the family's belt an extra notch and use the money to give the kids the best possible education. That old-fashioned family attitude toward education is what got many of our nation's most successful men and women their start in life.

Increasingly, there is another option of special interest to Retroculture people: home schooling. More and more mothers are teaching their children at home. It didn't used to be legal, but now it is in a growing number of states. A regular home schooling movement has grown up, with special courses and textbooks that teach mothers how to instruct their children along traditional lines. Through home schooling, the Retro family can be sure that its values and standards continue to shape their children as they learn academic subjects. The home school can actually use the old textbooks, like McGuffy readers. It can introduce children to classic literature for kids, from Beatrix Potter's *Peter Rabbit* through Jules Verne's *Michael Strogoff, Courier of the Tsar*, instead of the insipid "readers" used in most public schools. Home schooling is another benefit made possible if mom stays home with the children instead of going into the workplace — an extra dividend that makes the economic sacrifice involved all the more worthwhile.

As Retroculture grows and spreads and old standards are revived, the public schools may be able to become again what they once were, good, sound schools where parents can send their children without fear. In the meantime, Retro-families do face a challenge when it comes to finding a good school. But here as elsewhere, families grow stronger when they face and master challenges together. The sacrifices involved help the family become closer, as mother, father and children all work together in the same cause, the cause of recovering the good things we used to have.

THE RETRO-FAMILY AND CHURCH

Generally, Retro-families will want to go to church or synagogue. Of course, you don't have to be religious to adopt a Retroculture lifestyle. But it is a fact that religious belief and regular worship played large roles in the lives of most Americans through most of our history. It is difficult to understand the Victorians, for example, without realizing how important the church was for them. The strength of their families, their high moral purpose and their reforming zeal were intimately bound up with their religious beliefs and observances.

Even if you are not personally religious, you may want to give some thought to attending church. Church provides a time when we can renew our moral purpose, reflect seriously on our lives, and get some sound ideas on self-improvement. It brings the family together on a regular basis, week by week, in an atmosphere conducive to love, commitment, and the spirit of service to others families need to be strong. It ties us together with our forefathers in ways nothing else can. As we sing the same hymns they sang, experience the same emotions, and remember them praying perhaps in the very same church, we truly share a portion of their lives. We are engaging in what was, for many of them, the most important and meaningful action they took. It is easy to imagine them right there beside us… as, perhaps, they are.

Retroculture urges us not to be afraid of religious feelings. Often, the modern world presents religion almost as something evil or dangerous, a force that will make us narrow and mean. But if we just think of our own grandparents, who were probably believers and churchgoers, we see that is not so. They and their friends and neighbors, church members all, were kind, decent people. And they would have been the first to tell us that they owed many of their good qualities to what they heard in church. So even if you are not yourself religious, don't be afraid to go to church. It won't hurt you. And if, as you attend, you find your own religious feelings growing, let them.

If you are already a religious believer, Retroculture also has a message from the past for you. Go to church regularly, every Sunday, not just now and then. Many modern church members go on Christmas, Easter, and perhaps now and then the rest of the year. Our ancestors took their religious faith more seriously. They made their church a major part of their lives. They went every Sunday, they involved themselves in other church activities, they often made heavy financial sacrifices for their church (just look at the churches they built in your community; they weren't cheap!), and they often had home religious observances, morning or evening prayer and grace before meals, as well.

As the Bible says, "Go thou and do likewise." Church can only play the same role in our lives and in the lives of our families that it played for our forefathers if our commitment to it matches theirs.

The church can also help strengthen the Retro-family because a church is a family. It is a gathering of people who share some very important views. That gives members of a church a wide common ground, a basis on which they can comfortably interact with each other. Sunday school, the church Women's League, Bible study groups, altar guilds, church suppers and picnics all offer your family a chance to get together with other families with whom you have a lot in common. Part of that common belief in almost all churches is a strong belief in the family itself. When your family is in trouble, the other families in your church are there to help. When your family wants to celebrate, they are happy to join in. And when you want a safe, healthy environment for your children to play and learn in, you can find it in your church, because the other families there share your beliefs and moral values.

As a Retro-family, you may want to go beyond belonging to just any church; you may want to find a Retro-church. In recent years, many churches have drifted away from traditional theology and rites of worship. In the process, they have lost much of the old beauty of worship services and the power of traditional belief to help troubled souls. Fortunately, Retro-churches are not too hard to find. Some churches, such as those of Protestant Evangelicals, emphasize the "old time religion" just as it was preached to our grandparents and great-grandparents. In denominations like the Episcopalians that have jettisoned much of their beautiful traditional liturgy in recent years, along with traditional Christian theology, "continuing Churches" such as the Anglican Catholic Church still offer the old truths and church services. Some Catholic churches are again offering a Latin mass, with the Vatican's approval, and Eastern Orthodox churches have remained almost unchanged in belief and worship for a thousand years and more. If you are looking for a church where you can believe and worship the same way your ancestors did, you will probably be able to find one somewhere in your community.

In these troubled times, church is the first line of defense for the Retro-family. It is dedicated to the things families most need and want: sound moral values, good personal behavior, and strong belief in the importance of the family itself. If offers a place of refuge and shelter from the stress, rudeness, immorality and even danger that now beset our lives. Through the church, you can find a safe and wholesome setting for your family to grow, a community you can feel comfortable in. Take the advice your grandparents would certainly give you, and take your family to church.

LIVING THE RETRO LIFE ALONE

You don't have to have a family to live a Retroculture life. Just as the past offers useful patterns for a family to follow, so it offers the same to the single person. The Victorian bachelor, the maiden aunt, the spinster schoolteacher, all have something to say to today's single person.

The lives of single people in the past differed in some important ways from the single lifestyle that has become fashionable since the mid-1960s. In recent times, the single life has become identified with the "swinger," a person who lives largely for immediate pleasure. The advantages of being single are usually presented in terms of materialism, consumerism, and sexual "liberation." The single man or woman is seen to have more money to spend on themselves—fancy sports cars (no need for a van to haul the kids around), a luxurious apartment (no need for a yard for kids to play in), and vacations at Club Med (no need to save to put kids through college). They are also seen as free from the moral bonds of family, so they can "play around" with casual liaisons, cruise singles bars and "enjoy" an endless series of short-term relationships.

When this vision of single living was put forward in the 1960s as the "Playboy philosophy," many people found it attractive. And for a short time, it was. But as a philosophy of life, it left out one important fact: the aging process. As the playboys and playgirls of the 1960s hit their forties, then their fifties, they discovered that what works when you're young doesn't work well at all when you get old. Now, they find those short-term relationships hard to come by; it seems the other people in the singles bars want someone in their twenties, not their sixties. The sports car feels increasingly uncomfortable, the "bachelor pad" silently mocks the lonely nights, and wandering around the beach in a bathing suit brings more pitying than admiring looks.

When we think back to the single people of our grandparents' generation that we knew, we remember something different. Middle and old age seemed to sit comfortably on them. They weren't washed up at fifty. Their lives seem to have been built on something more solid than the foxfire of "eternal youth." What did they do differently that enabled them to live satisfying single lives?

One of the most important differences is that single people in the past usually dedicated their lives to service, not to personal pleasure. The Victorian bachelor was often dedicated to public service, in the diplomatic corps, the military, or as a political reformer. Many also built their lives around service as educators; university professors and serious writers were often bachelors. Others were artists, or explorers, or inventors. There were bachelor farmers, dedicated to their land, and bachelor craftsmen, their lives devoted to excellence in their craft.

The same was true of single women. One of the images of the past that most readily comes to mind is of the spinster schoolteacher. Much of our traditional (and now lost) excellence in public education was due to single women who as teachers devoted their lives to their pupils. And what splendid teachers they often were! Living on but small salary, they had little to spend but themselves. But of that they gave freely and bounteously. How many Americans now in their middle and later years remember their "Miss Canfield,"[8] to whom they owe their ability to read easily and with pleasure or figure more quickly in their head than their grandchildren can on a calculator. Nor was schoolteacher the only position in which single women served importantly. The school or town nurse everyone depended on, the librarian who personally knew the merits of each book in her library, the woman who for decades ran the excellent local hotel dining room, all these were important members of their community.

Unlike a life built on pleasure, a life built on service gets richer, not poorer, with age. Gradually the gratifying results of labor become evident: pupils return as well-educated men and women, leaders of the town; books are written that revolutionize their field and make their author famous; battles are won, treaties are written, a farm's land

---

8 A fictional character from the US sitcom *Leave it to Beaver*, which ran from 1957 to 1963, Miss Canfield was a young, pretty schoolteacher, whose name became a by-word for the archetypal caring teacher.

grows lush from tender care. The years bring the satisfaction of purposes accomplished and well-earned honors bestowed.

This, then, is the first word Retroculture speaks to single men and women today: service. Service, not self, is the basis of a full, satisfying single life. The Victorians were right and Hugh Hefner was wrong. The playboy becomes the sad and lonely aging man, a figure of pity or of fun. The faithful servant, of his or her nation, community, workplace, or family, grows in stature and honor and satisfaction with the years. On such is a solid and rewarding single life built.

Through service, the Retroculture single person does not live alone. He or she may have their own dwelling, but their lives are closely enmeshed with the lives of their family, colleagues and neighbors. Often, as aunts and uncles, single people in the past were important, active members of their family. They helped out when brothers or sisters were sick. They took care of nieces and nephews who needed care their homes could not offer. They paid the bills of family thrown out of work and put other family members through college. They regularly and frequently visited and were visited by their extended family.

Similarly, their service in their workplace and community ensured they did not live alone. Honored where they worked, their colleagues and others in their profession sought their company. They were busy in evenings on church and neighborhood committees. They were the backbone of community volunteer efforts. They served, because they had the time, as aldermen and vestrymen and Red Cross chairwomen.

Retroculture recommends single people today revive that old tradition of service to family and community. There are lots of people out there who need your help. Far better and more rewarding an evening with the hospital volunteers or the neighborhood association than one spent cruising bars. In return, you will find your life filled with the lives of others.

Retroculture's suggestion that the single person orient their life toward service, rather than self, points to another major difference between the playboy and the single person of the past. The playboy follows very different morals from the family man. In contrast, the single man or woman of the past followed the same moral code as married people. That made them acceptable, compatible members of their family and community. They didn't live much differently from other people.

By living a life similar to that of married people, the Retroculture single person today can integrate himself or herself into family and community. One possibility to think about that is helpful in doing this is owning a house. A house anchors a person. Working in the garden, keeping the house up (or restoring a neglected older house), cooperating actively with the neighbors to keep the community safe and orderly, all provide healthy and rewarding alternatives to the life of the "swinger." They tie the single person in with other people who are living solid, moral lives. (And, of course, involvement in the church is especially helpful.) All these provide an active social life that is not focused on youth, beauty and sex, the false lures of the single life. They tie the single man or woman into the shared values of the community, instead of cutting them off.

And Retroculture itself has a great deal of value to offer the single person. The Retroculture life is oriented not toward what can appear a bleak future, where age is the unbeatable foe, but toward a rich past that never loses its richness. Family history allows the family to grow rather than shrink with time. The greater resources which often accompany being single can create real wealth when devoted to restoration and preservation. Local history anchors the single person in the community and makes them a sought-after resource. Single people are well positioned to be pioneers of Retroculture, helping those around them to see the good in looking toward the past for guidance and also showing them where and how to find it.

RETROCULTURE AND YOUR LIFE

As this chapter suggests, whether you are single or married, Retroculture offers you more than just outward appearances. The past Retroculture seeks to recapture was not made simply out of Victorian houses and hats. The morals, values, and ways of living our forefathers followed, not just things, were what gave them solid, rewarding, happy lives. Retroculture seeks to recapture those old-fashioned ways of believing and behaving just as much as it seeks Victorian homes or safe, well-ordered 1950s suburbs. In fact, it is the need to get back to these basics of the good life that is the real reason Retroculture is growing.

FIGURE 4. Gibson Girls.
(Source: Illustration by Charles Dana Gibson, c. 1900)

CHAPTER VI

൭

Retro-Clothing

THERE IS NO QUESTION THAT IN THE PAST, people dressed better than they do today. What could be more elegant than men's dress of the 18th century, with richly colored waistcoats, knee-breeches and high silk stockings, all topped off with a powdered wig? Or, for women, what could surpass the "Gibson Girl"[9] of the late-19th and early-20th centuries, the time of tiny waists and enormous hats, flowing dresses and flowing tresses?

But recognizing the beauty of earlier clothing styles is one thing; wanting to wear them is something else again. Let's face it, clothing of earlier eras was not overly convenient. Powdered wigs and high neckstocks, corsets and bustles, veils and petticoats, top hats and spats all took a considerable amount of time to dress in and were not always comfortable. Few ladies will look forward to being laced so tightly into stays that they are prone to fainting, and few gentlemen will have the time to make a proper Edwardian toilette every morning.

---

9 A "Gibson Girl" was a personification of the fashion ideals from the late-19th and early-20th centuries, created by artist Charles Dana Gibson. She would be dressed in the latest fashions, and was depicted as calm, independent and beautiful. Such was her popularity that she appeared on numerous pieces of merchandise. She fell from favor with the arrival of more practical fashions during World War I, rather than the dresses, bustle gowns and shirtwaists favored by the Gibson Girl. — Editor.

...ng is something of a specialized interest even ..., many people would like to be able to recapture ...ce, style, and panache of dress in earlier times. We ... of the way "downtown" looked in the 1930s and we ...ifference clothing made. The men are mostly in styl... ...1 double-breasted, and every one of them is wearing a ... sort; no jogging suits or cut-off jeans here. Women are ..., pumps, hats, and often gloves. They make the whole town ...etter, and they look better themselves — better, we must admit, ...an we often look when we go downtown. Nowadays people even wear blue jeans and tee shirts to church, for Heaven's sake! Surely, there must be a way to dress ourselves and our communities up a bit without being uncomfortable, taking hours to dress or spending a fortune on our wardrobes.

Well, there is. In fact, there are several ways. They do not go to extremes, they do not make you stand out in ways you'd rather not, and they don't cost a fortune either. They do draw on the past, like all Retroculture, to give a "feel" of style, of care with how one appears, and a bit of the grace we wistfully admire in those wonderful old photos.

DRESSING UP

An easy place to start in dressing Retro is with the old-fashioned notion of "dressing up." It is perfectly all right to wear grubby old things, sweatshirts and cut-offs and tennis shoes and the like, to work in the garden, clean the house, wash the car, and even run down to the 7-11 for a quart of milk when you've run out. But when it's time to go downtown, or out to lunch, or even down to the mall to shop, perhaps it's time to stop a moment and take a quick look in the mirror. If you had to ask someone for directions, would they think they were being approached by a street person looking for a handout? If so, ask yourself another question: Is this one of those cases where mom or dad or nana would have dressed up a bit before leaving the house? If the answer is yes, you may want to do likewise. Dressing up need not involve suits or pumps or dresses; just do as most Europeans do and slip on a jacket if you're a man, or perhaps, if you're a woman, a skirt and sandals instead of sweat pants and jogging shoes.

Dressing up, which really just means dressing for the occasion, is one of those nice old notions we somehow lost in the last sixty years. It doesn't take special clothes or a great deal of time, just a bit of forethought about where you are going and how you yourself, by the way you dress, might brighten that place up a bit. Our grandparents too wore their grubbies around the house; remember how granddad always took his white shirt off when he got home and, at least on hot summer evenings, sat on the porch in his undershirt? The difference is, he would not have gone into town that way. That's really all dressing up means. It's one of the easiest ways to revive old ideas about style.

THE RETRO LOOK

As we've said before, there is no "correct" period for Retroculture; any time before the 1960s, when everything fell apart, counts as Retro. When it comes to clothing, however, most people who want to dress Retro will probably look toward the 1930s, 40s and 50s. This may apply even to Retro people whose own period is earlier than those years. Finding or making clothes that reflect the Edwardian, Victorian, or Colonial eras is a highly-specialized interest — one, to be sure, some folks will want to pursue, and we'll talk about it a bit further on. But clothes from those eras do require a special effort to find, they are not always terribly practical (Gibson Girls did not have to fit in Honda Civics), and they may make you stand out in the crowd more than you really care to.

Yet at the same time, you would like to distance yourself from the general modern slovenliness. You would like to look Retro without going to extremes and without being impractical. How to do it? The clothes from the 1930s, 40s, and 50s offer a perfect answer. They are not that different from what people are wearing today — in fact some are rapidly coming back into fashion. They are practical and comfortable. And no one is likely to think you are on your way to a costume ball. You can wear them to the office, to church, on a picnic or to school. Wherever you do wear them, you will let people know, in a subtle and gracious way, that you are one of those happy souls who look to the past for their future.

In clothing as in everything, Retroculture people are not spendthrifts. Dressing Retro does not mean throwing away your current wardrobe and spending a bundle on lots of new expensive clothes. Rather, the goal is the general look and feel of older times, particularly the years stretching from the 1930s through the 50s. If you think of clothing from those years as a generalized "Retro Look," you will see there's a great deal you can do to create that look without spending a fortune. Let's examine some of them.

NEW OLD CLOTHES

Every now and then, we all have to buy some new clothes. (If we're men, we usually hate it, but we're getting that "get away from me you bum" look on the Metro and it's time.) From the Retroculture viewpoint, the nice news is that more and more new clothes look like they were made in the 1930s, 40s or 50s. Just look through some of the style magazines: the ads show men in brown or tan double-breasted suits, sometimes with two-toned shoes, floral ties, and, yes, even hats again (that hole in the ozone layer is getting quite a few people thinking about hats). Women — when discussing Retroculture, we may speak of Ladies — are also wearing hats, nice big straw hats for summer, and they are carrying small purses too ("the ladylike handbag," says *Vogue*). The "Spring Ensemble" is back, especially for young women. Lanz advertises the floral print dress as "An American Classic."

When you have to get new clothes anyway, why not get these new old clothes? They don't cost more than any other new clothes and they put you at the leading edge of fashion at the same time they are old fashioned. What more could a Retro-person ask for?

That's fine for when we want to dress up, you might say, but what about casual clothes? Are those going Retro too? Here, Retroculture has a little trick to play, one that serves the fine old Retro-virtue of frugality. In the past, people didn't dress as casually as they do today. In the 1930s, for example, casual dress meant a sport coat, perhaps worn with a turtleneck instead of a shirt and tie, or a blouse and skirt instead of a dress. You can save some pennies for your old-fashioned piggy bank if you do the same, simply by taking dress clothes that are a bit too far past their best for church or work and making them your casual clothes.

Men's sport coats and slacks, or even jackets and pants from a suit (depending on the suit, of course) that aren't quite good enough for the office any more will make you look dressed up indeed (and very Retro) for a walk in the country or a trip into town to shop. You needn't worry about getting your "good" clothes dirty, because they aren't your good clothes any more. What was a sports jacket is now a "walking coat," a light jacket for those chilly mornings at the cabin in the mountains or on the beach. And, they're free! If you had bought casual clothes instead, the old good clothes would have gone to the Salvation Army or the rag man.

Ladies may have less opportunity to recycle their dress clothes this way; they are, and should be, more particular about their clothes than men. But they too may find ways to reuse clothes. Remember how many uses grandma got from what was originally her "Christmas dress?" (The last time we saw it, it had been transformed into curtains for the back windows on the third floor.)

If you want to buy new casual clothes that are Retro, you can. In Chapter One we pointed to the catalogue of the J. Peterman Company as one source for them; the Vermont Country Store catalogue is another. But "waste not, want not" is a good old Retro saying; why waste those past-their-best dress clothes when they make perfectly good casual clothes at no extra charge — and make you look nicely old-fashioned in the bargain?

RETRO ACCESSORIES

Modern dress clothes are not all that different from those of the 30s, 40s, and 50s. You can use the clothes you have to create a Retro look simply by accompanying them with some Retro accessories.

One of the easiest, least expensive and most effective is a hat. Hats have an almost magic touch; put one on with your usual suit and presto! You've gone back in time. No lady or gentleman would have gone out without a hat until the 1960s, which means that simply by wearing one, you have gone back before that slum of a decade. Nor have hat styles changed much. In fact, in the family attic or the used clothing shop you may easily find a hat from earlier years that works just as well today. Hats are not terribly expensive; less than $100 will get a man a good fedora or trilby he can wear with any suit or jacket. And hats look good. If you wear one, you will find you get admiring glances from the yet-hatless, glances that recognize a touch of class. In the summer, you will find that our ancestors were no fools; you are cooler with a light straw hat than you are going hatless. And there is that talk about the ozone layer…

For a slightly greater investment, you can build a modest inventory of headgear that permits some finer touches. Going to an important meeting at the bank in your best dark three-piece suit? Add a homburg and your fellows will think you're with J.P. Morgan. Getting out your best ensemble for church on Easter Sunday? Wear a hat with a veil. Taking that slightly worn camels' hair jacket on a ramble in the country? Top it off with a matching cap. In each instance, you will be at the top of fashion, simply by wearing just what your grandmother or grandfather wore on their heads for similar occasions.

Ladies have a special advantage when comes to taking their current wardrobes Retro with Retro accessories, simply because they have more of them. The small purse, especially if it is white, sends a message. So even more do gloves. Cosmetics should not be forgotten, either; that red Red RED lipstick of the 1940s has come around again (as most things do). Mother's or Grandmother's watch adds another Retro touch, and wouldn't she be glad to know you are wearing it. Jewelry from the past is very fashionable, and the family jewelry box may offer a good supply gratis. Older hair styles do wonders to create a Retro feeling, and they are coming back.

But there are Retro accessories for men, too, beyond just hats. Antique watches and new ones made to 1930s styles are now the height of fashion. Or you can go fashion one better by wearing granddad's pocket watch and watch-chain with that three-piece suit. Wear a sweater vest with a two-piece suit and welcome Fall in warmth as well as style. Bow ties are especially nice in Summer; try one with your Panama hat and Haspell summer suit (something that hasn't changed in eons). Comfortable walking shoes with soft cushioned soles now come in very traditional styles, so you can walk around town or country in comfort yet Retro-shod. Glasses frames from the 30s and 40s are very "in," and your local frame shop probably stocks them. Men's haircuts haven't changed much over the years (except when they simply got sloppy in the 60s and 70s), and a pleasant way to get a good old-fashioned haircut is to go to a real barber shop instead of a "hair boutique." A few survived in most places ~ check an old-fashioned strip shopping center or nearby small town — and they'll also save you money. Add some Brylcream ("A Little Dab'll Do Ya")[10] for a really Retro look. And what about the classic breast-pocket handkerchief or even a boutonniere? They will turn even the most modern suit Retro at a stroke.

Just as when you furnish your house Retro, when you dress Retro you should not fear to mix and match. You are not creating a museum

---

10 This was the classic advertizing slogan of the brand in their 1950s television adverts. — Editor.

exhibit, but a look: a look that says FDR or Ikeis in the White House,[11] the world is still in good order, and you're part of it. It's not a strange look. In fact, it's quite stylish, and it doesn't require anything really out of the ordinary. You can find it all in most good shops. You can wear it proudly anywhere, and be among the setters of fashion. It makes you look good, it makes wherever you are look better, and by mixing Retro accessories with your present wardrobe, you can do it with but a modest investment. In other words, it has all the Retro virtues.

There is one thing you can add to your Retro clothes and accessories, something that costs nothing at all but does make a difference: we might call it Retro-deportment. In times past, like the 18th century, there was an elaborate art of deportment for both men and women. As a young lady or gentleman, you learned just how to sit, stand, walk, reach and move. Every gesture was carefully controlled, to lend grace, style, and beauty, and to send a message that you were indeed a lady or gentleman, not Flossy the goat-herd or Jack the rag-man. Most of this has been lost, and few people today would have the time to revive it in its colonial-era elaboration.

But some of it was still with us until recently, up through our grandparents' generation at least. And that more modest, simpler version is worth considering. Remember how grandma told you to sit up straight and not sprawl, or, when you were a young lady, that young ladies crossed their ankles, not their legs? Or the slight bow a gentleman was to make as he held a door for a lady? Or at least not to chew gum or tend to itches in public? These modest and not overly burdensome rules of deportment are a nice accompaniment to Retro-clothing. They add a subtle message about the person who is wearing the clothes, a suggestion that the elegance of dress is at least skin deep.

---

11 The author is referring to Franklin D. Roosevelt (US president from 1933 — 1945) and David "Ike" Eisenhower (US president from 1953 — 1961), respectively. — Editor.

RETRO-SHOPPING, OR MAKING A CHORE A PLEASURE

Some people like to shop, and some (enlightened) shops make shopping a pleasure even for those who normally don't like it. But let's face it, in recent decades clothes shopping has tended to become a chore. It used to be you went to nice small shops where your family had gone for years, maybe generations. The people there knew their stock, liked their work, and also knew you. They took pride in fitting you out nicely in quality clothes and helping you enjoy the time you were with them: though you left some money behind, you knew you had gotten good value. They smiled with satisfaction when they met you on the street, still wearing the suit they sold you twenty-five years before.

Thanks to the evil twins that have afflicted haberdashery and millinery, the discount store and the boutique, shopping for clothes has become drudgery for most of us. The discount store is cheap, but shopping there is depressing and frustrating: the help is ignorant (if you can find any), the quality uncertain at best, and let's face it, most discount stores have an, ahem, aroma. The boutique is cute and the help usually eager (though here too often ignorant), but the prices are through the ceiling. Truth be told, the quality is often suspect as well: junk with small quadrupeds or kumquats or whatever on it as a "designer label" is still junk.

What is a Retro-shopper to do? Again, our ancestors offer us a suggestion: buy fewer but better things. Just as previous generations lived quite comfortably in smaller houses, so they generally also had smaller wardrobes. They got top-quality clothes, then made them last, often for a lifetime. One student at Princeton told how his father, also a Princeton man, went to London's Savile Row upon his graduation in 1929 and bought six suits. They were the only suits he ever bought, and they served him quite nicely through his whole career in the Foreign Service.

Retro before his time, this diplomat discovered something that can help all Retroculture people escape the expense and irritation of frequent clothes-buying: Retro styles never change. If you buy clothes that reflect the classic Retro look, you can happily ignore all the minor perturbations of fashion. Lapels shrink and grow, shoulders fatten and slim, and the fashion trade tries to make a big deal of it all. In fact, its piffle. When the Princeton man wore one of his 1929 suits to a diplomatic function in the 1960s, he looked distinguished, because the quality of his clothes was superb. He knew that wearing something too old to be quite fashionable is a mark of a gentleman, just as gentlemen tend to drive old cars and have old dogs. The same is true for ladies: that suit bought by Nana in Paris in 1935 and kept in perfect condition will make Madame the envy of the garden party today. Retro is forever.

By needing fewer things, you can also frequent better shops when you buy, thus avoiding the degradation of the discount house and the silliness of the boutique. Better does not mean slicker: the slick places, where everything is just-too-perfect and the help keep their noses in the air, are where the *nouveau riche* go to throw money around. In contrast, a really good clothing store tells you it's been there a while. It looks *echt*—that wonderful if untranslatable German word that rolls together real, genuine, unpretentious, established, the difference between the corner tavern and the fern-bar. Most cities and a good number of towns have at least one such clothing establishment. It's been there forever. The linoleum on the floor is a bit worn and the tin ceiling is original. The help is often elderly—the last of the real professionals in their trade. The hat department held on through the hatless late-20th century. They have three-button suits and bow ties. The prices are not cheap, but you get real value, good American and British stuff, not some wog creation that makes you look like a pimp on the *Via Veneto*. Your grandfather may have shopped there, and he may have had the same salesman. He would, without blinking, have bought the same suit.

Retro-shopping for the classic Retro-look at least minimizes the discomfort many gentleman face when it is time for new clothes.

Buying them under these circumstances, if not a giddy pleasure, at least feels right. And because the Retro-look is eternal, shopping is not something you must face often. Once you have the basics of your Retro-wardrobe, you are pretty much set for life. You can happily ignore changes in fashion: you're in the style you want for the rest of your days.

Ladies, or some of them, actually like to shop, we know. That is one of those mysteries of the feminine life that a gentleman can do nothing but pass over in silence and in awe.

PERIOD CLOTHING: GOING ALL THE WAY

Just as some Retro people will have no interest in Retro-clothing, others will have a great deal. They will want to go beyond the generalized Retro look, the styles of the 30s, 40s and 50s, and get clothing like that worn in their particular period. They may want to wear it for special events at home, like the Victorian family we met in Chapter I; for gatherings like reenactments of historic events; for club meetings with others who share an interest in their era; or just for the fun of it. A few brave souls may even wear it everywhere, and bully for them! They can serve as a silent reproach to all those people jogging in their underwear.

It may surprise some to discover that there are already whole cottage industries supplying a wide variety of period clothing and, even more, patterns from which such clothing can be sewn. They tend to fall into three general periods: late Victorian/Edwardian, Civil War Era, and colonial. Most sales are through catalogues, though you can also find a few stores (usually a catalogue headquarters).

A good example of what is available is the catalogue of "Amazon Vinegar & Pickling Works Drygoods (Purveyors of Items for the 19th-Century Impressions)," of Davenport Iowa. The offer a pattern catalogue: "Over 700 historic and ethnic clothing patterns are shown in an illustrated catalogue for the seamstress and tailor — for men, women and children. The years 1390–1950+ are covered with most emphasis on the 1800s (19th century). Everything from outer-garments (coats and cloaks), to undergarments (corsets and lingerie, underwear); from top (hats and bonnets) to toe (dancing slippers)." They also offer an extensive catalogue of ready-to-order items, including reproductions of period fashion books (*Fashions and Costumes from Godey's Lady's Book*), modern books on old fashions (*Victorians Unbuttoned!*) ladies high-buttoned shoes, corsets, yard goods made to antique styles (tulle with silver glitter: "In 1865 Empress Elizabeth of Austria was painted by Winterhalter wearing a Ball Gown of Glitter Tulle"), hoopskirts, a wide variety of wonderful hats including an Abe Lincoln Stovepipe, men's shirts with paper collars, books of etiquette (a family favorite, not offered here, is the 1870s *Don't* book, e.g., "Don't spit out of the train window; those riding behind you will wish you were under the wheels"), Civil-war era games and toys—in short, everything you need for a proper Victorian life.

The introduction to the catalogue by the woman who runs Amazon Drygoods offers an insight into the larger Retroculture life. Janet Burgess writes:

> I would like to introduce myself to you. My profession has been fabric and color as an Interior Designer for 24 years and as an Associate Member of the American Society of Interior Designers. Prior to entering the design field time was spent as a clothing designer, theatrical producer and freelance artist. I am listed in seven editions of 'Who's Who of American Women,' 'Who's Who in Finance and Industry,' and 'Who's Who in the Midwest.'
>
> I have a strong background in historic costume and am both a seamstress and tailor by avocation and education. I am restoring a house built in 1854 and have been active in the Village of East Davenport, Iowa's largest historic district, both as a charter Board Member and Past President for 12 years.
>
> Memberships include the Victorian Society of America and Iowa, the Costume Society of America, 16th Iowa Civil War Unit, the Midwest Open-air Museums Coordinating Council, the National Trust for Historic Preservation and a number of other historic preservation groups.

> The products of Amazon Drygoods are intended for a discriminating clientele who appreciate service & craftsmanship 100 years behind the times...

Similar sources can provide a wide variety of 18th-century clothing for those whose Retro-era is colonial. In areas like that around Washington, D.C., where interest in the colonial period is strong, there are local seamstresses who specialize in 18th-century clothing. You can also find clothing sources for the colonial era through places like Colonial Williamsburg and Plimouth Plantation in Plymouth, Massachusetts.

Those who want to go all the way with Retro-clothing are pioneering, but not in a barren landscape. You won't be alone. Like most hobbies, it is not inexpensive, but what you buy will be well made (most reproductions are sewn with fanatical attention to detail) and, of course, you need not concern yourself with changes of fashion. The future lies wholly, and securely, in the past.

AMAZING GRACE...

Whether you choose to go Retro a lot or only a little in the way you dress, you will find it the most personal way to set yourself apart from the crudeness of the early-21st century. You will bring into your own life, and the lives of all you meet, a hint of the grace, style, and propriety of earlier times. Even if you do nothing more than wear a proper hat, you will quietly, inoffensively signal your departure from the rampant ugliness of our time. There is, of course, no requirement that any of your clothing be Retro in order to live the Retro life. But Retro-clothing is one of the many gentle pleasures Retroculture offers. So, lie back in your hammock on a lazy afternoon, and think of how you might appear in a three-button suit with high paper collar and straw boater, or tight-wasted shirt, long flowing skirt and great Edwardian hat, and let your imagination lead you where it will.

FIGURE 5. Formal dinner party.
(Source: Sketch by Marguerite Martyn, *St. Louis Post-Dispatch*, 1920)

CHAPTER VII

〜

Retro-Entertainment

You have probably visited an old house, from the 17th, 18th or 19th century, that is now a museum. Perhaps you remember looking in the kitchen where museum staff were cooking old-fashioned dishes in front of an open fire or on a big black cast-iron stove. You saw the dining room, elegantly set for the kind of elaborate dinner our ancestors used to enjoy. You may have thought, "I wonder what it really would have been like to cook that way and sit down to such a dinner?"

A few years ago, a visitor to Colonial Williamsburg asked himself that question. And he decided to answer it. He found a colonial home, now a museum, that agreed to let him and a group of friends spend a day cooking 18th-century recipes in the original kitchen, in front of the open fire. He found a cooking teacher who had studied Colonial cooking and agreed to lead the group. They started at nine o'clock one Saturday morning, putting soup to boil over the open fire, shaping marzipan for a "hedgehog," and gathering herbs from the garden. At five that afternoon, they sat down to a three-course, twenty-three-dish 18th-century dinner in the elegant dining room of Belle Grove, a colonial plantation house near Winchester, Virginia. As they watched the daylight slowly fade over the beautiful Virginia countryside (every window in Belle Grove offers a glorious view) and the dining room take on the soft glow of candlelight, they realized they had come very close to spending a day in the 18th century.

The moral of this tale is that Retroculture offers an immense variety of entertaining things to do. It may require a bit of initiative on your part — Belle Grove had never done anything quite like this before — but if you push it a bit, the door to the past will swing open to reveal a wondrous landscape, filled with activities that are great fun. The Retroculture life is not one bit dull; on the contrary, it offers a much wider variety of entertainment than our own jaded age.

Of course, Retro-entertainment differs in some important ways from modern entertainment. Perhaps the most important difference is that it offers innocent rather than guilty pleasures. Modern entertainment is usually built around "shock effect," produced by degradation, sex and violence. We are supposed to be "entertained" by seeing and hearing things that, in real life, we would rather not hear or see and know we should not hear or see. Because this sort of entertainment quickly pales, the intensity of the shock must constantly be increased. So, television and video games grow ever more violent, movies and songs ever more prurient, until we finally gag — and thus, supposedly, are "entertained."

That is not how our ancestors sought entertainment. Of course, theater and music have always included some sex and some violence — just think of *Macbeth*, or *Electra*, or *The Marriage of Figaro*. But people did not go to see Shakespeare's *Macbeth* just to be shocked. They went for the depth of understanding of human nature Shakespeare presented, for what tragic theater said to all people about the nature of life, and for the magnificent artistry in the language and the portrayal, the arts of both playwright and actors.

For the most part, entertainment in the past was intended to be both pleasant and uplifting. People enjoyed splendid dinners, accompanied by serious and artful conversation; think of Dr. Johnson at the Literary Club in 18th-century London, or the table Jefferson presided over at Monticello. They enjoyed real music with wonderful tunes, music you could sing or dance to, or that called forth the highest talent of the greatest singers of their day. They read masterfully written novels, like those of Jane Austin, that also taught lessons about human nature. All these entertainments lifted people up above themselves, to see life in a new and clearer light.

Recovering uplifting entertainment may take some creativity and initiative on your part. The person who invited his friends to that 18th-century day in the kitchen and dining room at Belle Grove had the idea himself, then figured out how to make it happen. Once you start giving Retro-entertainment some thought, you too will find ways to make it happen. More and more people are doing so, in everything from amateur music groups that specialize in baroque music through model train clubs that have layouts for the old Lionel O-gauge and standard gauge "tinplate" trains. Old books, old films, old-fashioned dinner parties and picnics, are all coming back. It's part of the Retroculture trend, and it is making Retro-entertainment easier and easier to find.

Like other aspects of Retroculture, Retro-entertainment need not be terribly expensive. Some things are, of course; a week at the very Retro Homestead hotel in Virginia is not cheap. But a week at the even more Retro Chalfont Hotel in Cape May, New Jersey, is quite reasonable. You will easily be able to find or create Retro-entertainment to fit your budget.

Remember, Retroculture is itself entertainment. When you devote part of your life (or all of it) to recapturing the past, you will quickly find it entertaining. Furnishing your house Retro, dressing Retro, traveling Retro, are all fun. So are even such serious things as developing a strong, Retroculture family life. Going back to the past, wherever you choose to do it, is not a chore but a pleasure, even when it involves some work. It is the best kind of pleasure, one that calls for creativity, imagination, and involvement, instead of merely being a passive spectator holding some sort of electronic device.

Does that mean Retroculture forswears television, DVDs and the other electronic impedimenta of the present age? No. But it does mean Retroculture people approach them somewhat differently. Generally, we do not allow them to become substitutes for active, creative pleasures, as they have in the lives of those emblems of the early 21st century, the "couch potatoes." To see what we mean, and how Retroculture integrates modern devices with our desire to recapture the good things from the past, let us take a look at a common entertainment device, the television.

RETRO-TELEVISION

Reflecting Americans' growing interest in the past, some television networks are showing old programs. But even when the show is Retro, Retroculture people approach television with a degree of caution. The unfortunate fact is, television is not so much real entertainment as it is a sort of pacifier. It fills time, but instead of enlivening — as good entertainment always does — it deadens. The reason is simple: the television viewer's mind is inert. When you read a book or watch a play or engage in dinner table conversation, your mind has to be active. You must imagine the scenes in the book, or think about the play's message, or consider what to say next. In contrast, the television does it all for you, leaving you sitting there like a bowl of warm blancmange. In fact, you cannot stop and think or reflect, because the program moves relentlessly onward.

Retroculture people know that for something really to entertain, it has to spur activity, not halt it. So they resist becoming television addicts. They may watch television, but they select what they are going to watch. Life for them is more than plunking down after dinner and turning on the tube.

This is especially true of Retroculture families with children. Children are easily absorbed by television, but what does it do for them? Does it stimulate their imaginations, teach them how to think and be creative, how to talk or write to express themselves? The answer, for the most part, is no. Far better for them are coloring books, paint sets, board games and puzzles, books and sports and trips to the museum or the country. So, most Retroculture families limit television watching, and a growing number are giving up television entirely, at least while children are small. This helps create a truly old-fashioned home, where children have all the stimulation and interaction kids routinely got before television.

If you do decide to have a television, there are a growing number of Retroculture shows and programs you can watch. Public Broadcasting Service (PBS) generally offers the best. Recent examples include *Victoria and Albert* and *Downton Abbey*.

In cable television, the Retro influence is strong. With cable, we have in effect individualized television, to the point where Retroculture people may be able to integrate it with "their" era. The American Movie Channel, as one example, shows only old movies, from the 1920s through the 1950s. A number of cable networks, including *Nickelodeon* and *The Family Channel*, are broadcasting TV series from the 1950s and early 1960s. Bravo offers high culture, including the plays and operas many Retro people enjoy. And new cable channels are being created, some of which may be partly or wholly Retro.

Could we in the future see a channel that simply recreates 1950s TV, ads and all? It's quite possible. What about a channel for "Victorian Television" — TV as it might have been had the Victorians invented it, it could dramatize the novels of Henry James or non-fiction works like Nicolay's and Hay's biography of Lincoln: have a show devoted to the latest Victorian inventions like the trolley car and the phonograph and perhaps include *The Century Magazine*, a talk show devoted to the "hot" topics of the 1880s and 1890s. After all, someone has written a novel, *The Difference Engine*, that imagines the Victorians inventing the computer (steam-driven of course); why not television?

Before television, radio provided good family entertainment, and it can do so again. Unlike TV, radio requires an active mind on the part of the listener; it evokes images rather than providing them. And that can be powerful: the pictures we create in our own imaginations as we hear a radio show unfold may be more vivid than anything a television screen can provide.

Already, radio is offering more than just news and music. The Prairie Home Companion was a great success, offering a type of program, the variety show, that tends to be dull on TV. American Radio Theater does the same. Some of the old radio dramas from the 1930s and 40s, like *The Shadow* and *The Green Hornet*, are turning up again on local stations. Some stations offer "Old Fashioned Saturday Nights," with shows and music from the great days of radio.

Just as TV offers new opportunities for Retro-entertainment, so does radio. What about stations devoted *in toto* to re-creating the past, including news, ads, everything, so when you tune in you take a trip in your Retro time machine? It's not too far-fetched to imagine. In today's highly segmented market, a station can succeed by being the only one that caters to a certain specific market, and Retroculture people offer that kind of market. Think of being able to turn on your big RCA radio made in 1935, the kind with tubes and lots of knobs and dials, and hear exactly what you might have heard in 1935. Now that *would* be entertainment!

Film, television, the DVD, all were supposed to kill legitimate theater. It hasn't happened. On the contrary, live theater is gaining strength. More and more places have live theaters, and more and more people are going. They are finding that the immediacy of live theater is more powerful than even the best special effects in movies. While television is a "cool" medium, theater is a "hot" one. It conveys emotional intensity and involvement much better than television does. And people who have grown blasé in front of the tube find a play gripping and entrancing.

The live stage is also seeing period revivals, of both plays and musical productions. One very Retro young gentleman in Chicago writes:

There is a wonderful troupe here that puts on light opera, the sort of stuff which took Broadway by storm seventy years ago and which is not on videotape. I've seen Romberg's 'New Moon' with some wonderful tunes, Victor Herbert's 'The Red Mill,' Strauss's 'Fledermaus' and Gilbert and Sullivan. The ticket prices are very reasonable, and it is amazing to see how the old folks come out in droves to pack the auditorium for the performances. There are no empty seats at the beginning and few dry eyes at the end of the evening.

Sometimes, not only is a historic play or opera revived, it is presented as it would have been when it was first staged. A small opera company in Alexandria, Virginia, put on the famous 18th-century *Beggar's Opera* in historic Gadsby's Tavern, exactly as it might have been staged in Washington's time, including using candles for lighting. It was a great success. In London, Shakespeare's Globe Theater has been built just as it was in the 16th century to perform his plays exactly as they were offered then. These truly Retro entertainments are popular with a wide variety of people, and are a good introduction for "newcomers" to the pleasures Retroculture offers.

MAY I HAVE THIS DANCE?

What has happened to dancing in the last sixty years must make Fred Astaire glad he's dead. The grace, the art, the style, have all vanished; people just go out onto the dance floor and shake as if they had some regrettable nerve disorder or a particularly nasty insect in their underwear. The "music" suggests a New York subway train passing close at hand, with the addition of a monotonous heavy beat: the village idiot hammering on a washtub. The average "dance" makes a good approximation of Hell.

It used to be otherwise. Dancing required both grace and skill. You had to put some effort into it, learning steps which were often quite intricate. (Remember dancing classes? They were the first occasion where a young gentleman met a young lady without slipping a frog down her back.) And music for dancing was often splendid: think of Strauss's *Blue Danube* and *Vienna Woods*. When fine music and good dancers came together in a grand formal ball, a bit of Heaven was brought down to earth. Even in small towns, the hotels gave balls with good orchestras; grandmother wore her tiara, and grandfather a top hat and tails. The 1930s were the era of the great swing dance bands and evenings at the Avalon: Tommy Dorsey, Glenn Miller, and the jitterbug.

How sad it is that most young people today have no idea what a real dance is like. But with the growth of Retroculture, some are learning. Real dancing, with set steps, recognizable music and partners, is making a comeback. Square dancing and folk dancing are both real dancing, and they have already gained large followings. Ballroom dancing is gaining interest among college students, and all ages are enjoying a revival of big band "swing" music and the dances that go with it.

Can Retro-dance really recapture the glories of the grand ball? It's already happening. At Cincinnati's Flying Cloud Academy, students spend a week intensively studying period dance, including etiquette, fashions and even hairstyles appropriate to the grand ball. *Victoria* magazine writes:

> In a short time, dancers are transported back to an era when ballroom etiquette and strict decorum were *de rigueur*. As they perfect their mazurkas and quadrilles, they enjoy taking to heart Victorian admonishments that 'a gentleman should exercise the utmost delicacy in touching the waist of his partner' and 'a lady should consider herself engaged to her partner, and therefore not at liberty to hold flirtation, between figures, with other gentlemen.' Above all, students keenly await the climax of all their efforts — the Grand Ball, their chance to claim dance cards bearing this Victorian verse: 'Each was so happy/And All was so fair/That night stole away/And the dawn found them there.'

SHALL WE HAVE A MUSICALE?

The musicale was a nice Victorian entertainment from the days before the Victrola made music readily available in the home. It was simply a matinee or soiree where someone added live music to the usual entertainments of food, drink and conversation. Can you imagine holding a musicale in your home today, with the latest rock band providing the tunes? No? You'd rather not be sued by your close friends and dear relatives for costing them their hearing? We understand.

What has happened to music? Permit us a short, serious digression into musicology to answer that question. Music has two basic elements: structure (how the notes are put together) and dynamics (how much the volume changes). If we listen to music from the 17th and 18th centuries, we find that the emphasis is on structure, not dynamics. The structure is often very complex, requiring an educated and discerning ear to appreciate all that is going on — the sort of ear a nobleman might have possessed. That tied music and audience together nicely, since both composers and performers usually worked for noblemen. The composers were also tied to the instruments on which their music would be played: most baroque instruments had only a limited dynamic range.

Then, around the beginning of the 19th century, two changes took place. The composers and performers began to derive their incomes from performing for the public, not serving as members of a nobleman's household. And, new instruments were developed that had a much greater dynamic range. Think of the piano: its proper name is the "pianoforte," or the "soft-loud." That is because, unlike the harpsichord, when you hit the piano's keys softly, the resulting sounds are soft, and when you really bang on them, the sounds are *loud*. 19th-century composers put the mass audience together with the new instruments to produce a new musical style, the romantic, that simplified structure and emphasized dynamics. And that trend, continued, has given us the hideous noise that kids listen to at rock concerts. Are we saying that Wagner leads directly to Slayer? Well, yes.

The reason for this short lesson in music history is that it points out a happy Retro-fact: the only place for music to go is back. The emphasis on dynamics over structure has gone as far as it can go; any further leads to music indistinguishable from passing trains. Future music is going to have to swing the pendulum back toward structure. And guess what? That means we may again hear music that is actually pleasant to listen to.

Of course, you can already have such music simply by listening to old music. Every Retro era offers good music, from the great choral singing of the Civil War era through ragtime and jazz to the Beach Boys and the tuneful "soul" of the early 1960s. Some are very serious: amateur groups like Washington's "Wondrous Machine" go to great lengths to play Baroque music as it would originally have been heard, on period instruments. And from that height, good music may range right down to getting out grandmother's old Victrola and playing her 78's.

Nor is good music only to be found in the past. One glorious source of it remains alive, well, and productive: Broadway. Steven Sondheim is right up there with Victor Herbert when it comes to writing songs people can hum, whistle, sing, and enjoy. Broadway song writers and producers know that their audiences want enjoyable music, and that a show that fails to offer it will bomb. The same good *bürgerlich*[12] audience that kept the Romantic composers in wine and cheese has its limits, and atonality or the "wall of sound" exceeds them. That audience may have released the devil of dynamics, but it also wants him kept in check, so even in the musical desert of the 21st century a few flowers bloom, on Broadway of all places.

But Retroculture seeks more than seeing (or hearing) the past and enjoying the few remnants that remain alive. It wants to bring it back. And nowhere more than in music can Retroculture do that, with a bit of imagination. We have great compositions from past musical eras,

---

12 A German expression meaning middle-class or bourgeois. — Editor.

like the baroque or the classic. But why should we think that no more great pieces can be written in those styles? What might we hear if a rich patron, or a great university, or a grand orchestra held a contest to see who could write the best new symphony in the style of Haydn or *cantata* in the style of Bach? Or if Broadway put on a new musical written in the style of the 1920s? Or if someone put together a new big band of the sort Benny Goodman used to lead and offered new as well as old music written in the style of the 1930s?

There is no reason to believe the old styles have played themselves out. All that is needed is some Retro-imagination to crank them up again. How would people react? Well, Retro-people would react with great enthusiasm. And so, we predict, would many others who may not yet know that at least in music, they are Retro-people too.

ENTERTAINING AT HOME

Before "home entertainment centers" the home was an entertainment center. After all, what's the point in having a home if you're not going to use it as a place to entertain and be entertained? You may sleep and eat just as well in a boarding house (for you youngsters, that's where people who couldn't afford an apartment lived before we turned over our park benches and subway stations to them).

A proper Retro-home offers a thousand entertainments, from gardening and reading good books to simply enjoying the swing on the front porch on a languid summer evening. Junior may be playing with his Lionel electric trains in the basement while Mother does needlepoint in the parlor and Father enjoys a good Havana cigar in his den. Furthermore, if we look back to the happy years before television (and even radio), we find our ancestors had a great many entertaining home activities that, through Retroculture, we may care to revive.

One is the dinner party. The cocktail party, where people surreptitiously try to make a meal of *hors d'oeuvres* while pretending to enjoy superficial conversation with persons they've never met, is a regrettable modern invention. In the good old days, a party usually meant sitting down around a meal. And while the dinner party has not totally died out, it is useful to remind ourselves of its superiority. It allows for, and indeed requires, conversations both serious and amusing — that is an obligation on guests. It permits the hostess to use her best china and silver and trot out her family's favorite recipes. It provides a leisurely dinner — a great and welcome rarity these days. It permits people new to each other to do more than exchange views about the weather; through the course of a dinner party, you can usually tell whether you're dealing with a prospective friend or a hopeless bore. Old friendships renew easily, stimulated by the twin lubricants of mind and tongue, good food and good wine. If the cocktail party suggests sleazy Hollywood agents "networking" with one another, the dinner party brings to mind Masterpiece Theater.

Retroculture people can do more than give dinner parties; they can give Retro-dinner parties. Why not give the sort of 18th-century dinner mentioned at the outset of this chapter? You need not cook it in front of the fire; just use 18th-century recipes (a number of colonial cookbooks have been published) and serve *à la française*. where each course includes a number of dishes, rather than *à la russe*, where you get the soup, then the salad, then the main course, etc. Or you can serve a Victorian dinner, again with period recipes; if your guests are also into things Victorian, you may add Victorian dress and table manners. A bit of research will quickly show what was served and done at dinner parties in your era, whatever that may happen to be. What nicer way is there to go Retro?

Another pre-TV home entertainment was houseguests. Those who live in the country know how entertaining it can be to have someone from town for the weekend, to catch up on all the latest goings-on. These days, people seem to have the idea that, as host and hostess, they must devote themselves to their guests' every waking moment. Retro people know better. In the old days, guests were generally left to amuse themselves through the day, and everyone gathered at breakfast, at dinner, and in the evening. This makes visits easier on both hosts and guests, who in truth would usually prefer some time to themselves to relax. It also helps the guest fulfill his obligation, which is to be entertaining, something few people can manage every hour of the day. Approached Retro-style, having houseguests can again be the pleasure it once was, for all concerned.

Germans have an enjoyable old institution called the *Stammtisch* that we might with advantage import. Once a week or once a fortnight, a set group gathers at a certain restaurant or tavern, always at the same table. There, they eat, drink some good German beer, talk, and maybe play cards. This can as readily be done at home as at a restaurant, and is especially nice for single people. By providing a regular gathering — say, for brunch after church — such an informal "club" cuts through the isolation the single life can bring. Because the people are the same week by week, the *Stammtisch* becomes an on-going conversation, a chance for all to share their amusing or difficult experiences of the previous week with interested and sympathetic listeners. And the regularity of it offers just the sort of order and predictability Retro people like.

For families, one of the best home entertainments is the extended family gathering. Here all the family — parents, grandparents, aunts, uncles, cousins, and often family friends as well — come together for the sort of gargantuan meal that leaves everyone bloated, glassy-eyed and blissfully content. Holidays provide a good excuse, and it is easy to develop a regular round of holiday gatherings: aunt Emma's for Easter, cousin Bob's place in the country for the Fourth of July, your house for Thanksgiving and Grandma's for Christmas. Everyone brings enough food for themselves and at least a dozen other people, ensuring mounds of leftovers to be exchanged so no one has to cook for a week. All talk of diets is rigidly excluded, and for the day no such thing as cholesterol exists. By their very nature, such gatherings become Retro: everyone tells the old family stories, like about the time Cousin John, long deceased, suggested the finicky bishop suck a raw egg. The food is all the old favorites, and after dinner there may be slides or home movies that bring those family members now gone back to life. Seldom does a house become a home so much as when the whole extended family gathers in it to enjoy and reminisce.

Not all entertainments before television revolved around food (though it is true — and not a bad thing — that in many houses, the social center was the kitchen). Surprising as it may be to the video game generation, there were many entertaining games that did not and do not require electricity. There is a wide variety of board games and puzzles for all ages. Many, like Scrabble, are educational as well as entertaining. Some, such as backgammon, are making a comeback. And whatever happened to bridge club? All across America, as late as the 1950s and 60s, people gathered regularly to play bridge. If the club included gentlemen it usually met in the evenings; ladies gathered for bridge in the afternoon. The game moved house-to-house as each member of the club took their turn as host or hostess. A revival of bridge clubs would be the perfect symbol of Retro-entertainment; while the modern Home Entertainment Center caters to the passive mind, bridge requires a very active mind indeed — woe to the partner who misses a chance to trump!

The Retro-home is a lively home. There is always a lot going on there, and that is the secret of Retro home entertainment. Our ancestors looked for things to do that were entertaining; they did not just plunk down passively and wait to "be entertained." Once you start to look for the same thing, you will find your home offers a wide variety of interesting things you can do. Many of them are just what people used to do before life was supposed to come to us out of some electronic box. So, ditch the phone and discover how entertaining an active home life can be. Once the television, phone and computer have been silenced, you will discover your home has another, non-electronic window on the world: the front door. Outside that door lies a neighborhood where you may find a great many entertaining things to do. A good start is just walking to see your neighbors. If you know your neighbors, you will know which ones will welcome you just dropping in and which ones would prefer an arrangement in advance, if only a telephone call. If you don't know them, walking through the neighborhood is a good way to meet them. You'll often find them out cutting the grass or working in the garden or walking the dog, and quite happy to stop for a moment and make your acquaintance.

In the good old days, it was easier to walk around the neighborhood and socialize informally because in the evenings you would find most people sitting on the front porch. A modern-day event in one neighborhood re-created that situation, when an evening thunderstorm knocked out the electric power for a few hours. With the house dark, once the rain was over almost everybody came out and sat on their front porch or front steps, or walked around to chat with other families that were sitting out enjoying the unaccustomed quiet. For that one evening, the whole neighborhood went Retro, as people amused themselves in pre-electronic ways. And despite the worries about thawing freezers, everybody rather enjoyed it.

A good way to introduce neighbors to each other and pave the way for informal visits is to hold a block party. Usually it just takes one family that is willing to offer its back yard for the gathering and invite people; everyone is happy to come and bring food, chairs, tables etc. It can easily become an annual affair to which everyone looks forward as a chance to meet new neighbors and renew old acquaintances, and to get a taste of everyone else's prize casserole or cake.

In real neighborhoods, where people know each other and interact as they used to, individuals often develop a particular neighborhood "function." If you are retired and usually home, you may keep an eye on houses where the people are gone through the day, putting the paper in the front door when it comes late, signing for packages, and letting others know if some suspicious characters have been hanging around. If you have some teenage children, they may become the neighborhood lawn mowers. There is often a "green thumb" on the street everyone else can turn to for advice on gardening, and also a local mechanic who is happy to help when your car won't start. Sometimes you have the luck to have in residence one of those wonderful women who love to bake more than they can possibly eat and happily distribute the surplus to their neighbors. Younger people often are gladly willing to offer a helping hand to the elderly, especially those who are living alone. These functions or specialties not only benefit the whole neighborhood, they give you your particular place in it. And that is part of what makes a real neighborhood a fun place to live.

Beyond such informal neighborhood functions lie regular neighborhood organizations, block watches, neighborhood associations, historic districts and the like. More and more neighborhoods have such organizations, and while their work is serious, being involved in them is also entertaining in that their work is interesting and rewarding. They offer many opportunities for you to involve yourself in ways you find of interest: researching your neighborhood's history, representing its interests with town government, working with the police, even getting active in town politics. Remember, Retro-entertainment recognizes that serious pursuits can also be entertaining; in fact, they are often the best entertainment (just look at how seriously some people take their hobbies). Our forefathers were often heavily involved on a volunteer basis in building up their communities and neighborhoods, and they found much more personal pleasure in such work than we get from renting a movie.

From a Retrocultural standpoint, the greatest value in seeking entertainment in your neighborhood is that it helps make it a genuine neighborhood. Community is one of the most important Retro-values, because it is something our ancestors had and we have largely lost. It is one of the main reasons their lives seem so much fuller and more rewarding than our own. We can have it again, but only if we invest something of ourselves in re-creating it. Calling on the neighbors, getting up block parties, organizing a neighborhood watch—all these things help people in a neighborhood get to know each other and become a community. And life in a genuine community is entertaining, in many profound and meaningful ways.

"JOHNNY, YOU MUST LEARN TO ENTERTAIN YOURSELF"

In the old days, that was the speech children got when they complained they were bored. (Nowadays, too often they just get driven to the mall.) It was good advice. One of the things we often envy in our grandparents was that they were never bored, because they could always find something entertaining to do on their own. They had hobbies, they had gardens, they liked to bake or do needlework or build model ships that actually sailed (that was a big hobby in the 1930s; just look through some old *Popular Mechanics* magazines). Retroculture advises us, young or not so young, to recapture that ability to entertain ourselves.

There are as many ways to do it as there are human interests. But there are two that stand out in terms of what they offer the Retroculture life. The first is reading old books. When you read the books the people who lived in your favorite era read, you enter into their lives. You gain a pure, undiluted insight into their world. That is not to say that the books themselves (we are generally speaking of fiction here) offer an accurate portrait of life in that era, but rather that by reading what they read and being entertained by what entertained them, you enter into their lives. For example, let's say your first love is the Edwardian era. When you collect and read popular fiction of that time, books such as *The Prisoner of Zenda* or C.N. and A.M. Williamson's *The Lightning Conductor*, you gain a marvelous sense of the lightness, grace, and innocence of those years, the years immediately preceding the First World War. You enter into a world so confident that it could relax and laugh a bit at itself and accept a fabulous kingdom like Ruritania, as children are secure enough to accept the world of Peter Pan or Mary Poppins. Perhaps only thus, by returning to an age of innocence, can innocence be recaptured in lives long past childhood.

The next time you're out for a walk stop into a bookstore that specializes in old books and take one in hand, one from the time that means most to you. Gain the powerful sense of the past that comes just from opening it. Let the music of its antique phrases draw you into that lost world. Puzzle at first over what seem strange references to clean collars and Pullman tickets and baggage smashers and jockey-pulley levers on motor cars. Smile at the Princess Flavia just as your great-grandmother smiled at her. And find yourself quickly and totally lost in that bygone world.

There is only one thing that compares as Retro-entertainment with sitting back in your favorite chair in the most Retro room in your house on a rainy afternoon and reading a book from the past, and that is writing. Our ancestors read for entertainment, but they also wrote for entertainment. Just read some of their letters, letters from great men or women of the past collected in volumes and published, or letters from members of your own family now long departed. What a difference from a phone call or "email"! Letter writing was an art, and as all arts was done with practice and care. The result was pleasure for both parties, the writer and the reader.

Here Retroculture is winning at least a small victory, because in the face of all the hideous noise generated by electronic "communication," letter writing is staging a modest comeback. Sick of all the gadgets that beep and chime, a growing number of people, including young people, are again writing letters and even taking some time and care to make them entertaining and enlightening to read. And that, they are discovering, also makes them entertaining to write. Like most Retro-entertainments, letter writing takes some effort and demands mental activity, but Retroculture people recognize those as advantages, not drawbacks. Next time you are bored, instead of flipping through the channels, give letter writing a try. Take some nice paper and a fountain pen.

> My dearest Jane,
> It has been ever so long since I last wrote, but I have some thoughts I would like to share especially with you …

Nor is it only in letters that the entertainment of writing is being rediscovered. Diaries and journals are also making a comeback. Lucky the person today who can in later years bring youth back to life by reading his or her diary. Luckier still the person who has his great-grandfather's Civil War diary or grandmother's journal of life in the country. But it is not only reading diaries and journals that is entertaining; writing in them can also be a pleasure. When we keep a diary or journal, we take time to reflect each day on where we have been and where we are going. We have a brief time of communion with ourselves and our inmost thoughts. We put the day's events in a larger perspective, and thereby bring them into order. With thought of those who in future years may read our words, we consider how we may best express our ideas on paper so that we give to them, grandchildren and great-grandchildren we may never meet in this life, some insight into who we really were.

Just as with sewing or playing the piano, as we do more writing we get better at it. And that is part of the essence of Retro-entertainment: self-improvement. Real entertainment is watching ourselves grow. Writing about ourselves, not just the events in our lives but our thoughts and our emotions, is a powerful tool for growth. It was not for nothing that our Victorian forebears believed so strongly in self-improvement, and worked at it. It was through ceaseless personal growth they became the strong, wise and contented people we look back on with admiration. Much of that growth came from putting pen to paper.

PERIOD ENTERTAINMENTS

Nothing offers better entertainment for Retroculture people than an opportunity to step back into the past. Fortunately, such opportunities are becoming more numerous. With a bit of creativity and initiative, you may be able to create your very own "time machine." That is what the people mentioned at the beginning of this chapter did when they approached Belle Grove plantation with a proposal to prepare and then sit down to a genuine 18th-century dinner.

The fact that Belle Grove accepted their proposal illustrates a change in the way many museums operate. Instead of just being places to see, they are becoming places to do things. As a visitor, you may be invited to help cook in an antique kitchen, throw a switch on a steam railroad, work the bellows in a smithy or feed the chickens on a colonial farm. Visitors' participation in such routine, on-going museum activities is limited and carefully supervised, but it still offers more access to the past than mere watching. Some museums are doing still more, offering special events such as dances, dinners, harvest festivals and the like that replicate past events and that invite participation by outsiders.

Retroculture people may wish to go still further and join in museum activities on a regular basis as volunteers. This can be one of the most entertaining and rewarding ways of "living in the past." A wide variety of museums need and eagerly welcome volunteers: retired streetcar motormen and conductors run heritage trolley lines, housewives lead tours and run demonstration kitchens and gardens on colonial plantations, mechanics help fix up historic aircraft so they can fly again, and students assist in restoring Victorian resort hotels. Often, roles as volunteers include wearing period clothing, operating antique equipment, and even speaking old-fashioned English. Not only is all this great fun, it also offers an opportunity to meet other Retroculture people who share an interest in your particular era.

If you want to see just how far back volunteering can take you, pay a visit to Fort Henry in Canada, near Kingston, Ontario. Fort Henry was built in the early 19th century to defend Canada against a feared American attack. Today, it is garrisoned by a 19th-century British Army unit. The troops wear 19th-century uniforms perfect in every detail, right down to getting the same cloth made at the same factories in England. They walk, stand, march, and salute exactly as they would have more than 100 years ago — off duty as well as on. They even talk as they would have then. Every soldier virtually lives in the 19th-century British Army — and every one of them is a student volunteer.

You may also find people recreating the past without being connected to a specific museum or historic site. The best example is the many Civil War military units. Throughout the East, volunteers have re-formed historic units from the Civil War, Union and Confederate. They wear Civil war uniforms, practice Civil War military drill and tactics, and gather regularly to reenact battles and stage encampments. Often, whole families have gotten involved, with wives and children also joining in the encampments, dressed as they would have been in the 1860s and camping as they would have at that time. Many of them are fanatical about being historically correct in every detail of their clothing, equipment, and actions, right down to reading only books and magazines of the 1860s. You can easily find and visit one of their encampments or battle re-creations if you live east of the Mississippi, and there are a few units in the west as well. There are also some Revolutionary War units that do the same things.

Nor are military units the only volunteer groups devoted to living in the past. You may find antique car clubs where people dress in the styles popular when their car was manufactured and go on "motor tours" as they might have back then. There are groups that gather to re-create pioneer wagon trains. You can find clubs devoted to antique dance, music, and theater.

The possibilities are endless. All it takes is a bit of imagination and willingness to invest some time and effort. Think, for example, of what might be done at Colonial Williamsburg. It is a lovely place to visit, but when one is surrounded by tourists dressed in sneakers and shorts one does not really get the feeling of living in the 18th century. Suppose a group or club of people who really wanted to experience 18th-century life went to Williamsburg with this proposal: For two weeks, in the winter when few tourists come, close Williamsburg to the general public. Fill it instead with people who want to personally experience colonial life. They will all wear 18th-century dress. They will live in the restored houses and inns, exactly as they would have 200 years ago, sleeping on corn husk mattresses, using candles for light, cooking in front of open fires, and bathing in tin tubs set before the hearth. Compromises with modernity would be kept to the absolute minimum, e.g., emergency medical care. The group might even go so far as to restrict conversations to 18th-century topics, including the politics of the time, philosophical ideas then current, and the "latest" fashions from London. They might choose a specific two week period to re-create, say, two weeks in January of 1776, with the newspaper and debate in the House of Burgesses and around the dinner tables in the taverns centering on the events of those two weeks. It would be a "total immersion" program, just as when you study a language in classes where no English may be spoken.

Or what about doing a six week "internship" at Plimoth Plantation[13] in Massachusetts? Plimoth already goes to great lengths to reproduce 17th-century life, including using the language and discussing only the topics of that time. Perhaps a few houses could be set aside for interns, houses with no modern conveniences whatsoever, where a docent would provide a "total immersion" program in early-17th-century colonial life.

The only limits on what can be done in Retro-entertainment are those you set on yourself. Remember, you will be best entertained not by what is done for you, but by what you do. The more you pioneer, the more you create, the more you not just take the ball but make the ball and run with it, the more you will find your life entertaining, enriching, and rewarding.

---

13 This is a living history museum founded in 1947, replicating the original 17th-century Plymouth colony founded by the "Pilgrims." — Editor.

CHAPTER VIII

❧

Retro-Manners

AS THE FLOOD OF ALL THAT IS HIDEOUS and awful begins to recede, whom should we see emerging from amongst the wreckage, dry, prim, and proper, but Miss Manners? And a welcome sight she is. In the national survey mentioned earlier, 92% of those polled said we should turn back toward past manners — the highest percentage for any item surveyed.

It's no wonder. Manners, public and private, have become atrocious. People blare "their" music at everyone around them from "boom boxes," car radios or earphones turned up to the max, with no regard as to whether others share their musical taste. With their cellphones they hold private conversations in public places. They make engagements, then don't show up and neither explain nor apologize for the inconvenience they have caused. Men harass women, and women try to be "one of the boys" by using vocabularies that would embarrass a longshoreman. People in "service" industries routinely insult their customers; in fact, a whole industry — telemarketing — has been built around the rudeness of telephoning strangers in their homes (usually at the dinner hour) to sell things to them. Children behave like the young savages they naturally are with no rebuke from their parents and no instruction in better behavior. Anyone who objects to this ill-mannered assault is himself thought rude; it is as if etiquette's only commandment were to take whatever mud is thrown in your face silently and without complaint.

It used to be otherwise. People were expected to show consideration for others, whether around the family breakfast table or at a football game. Those who failed to do so, who did not "mind their manners," were politely but firmly reproved. If they persisted in vile behavior, they were excluded from good society.

When did we go wrong? As usual, the answer is in the cultural revolution of the 1960s. That revolution entailed a wholesale rejection of etiquette and manners, of all rules for behavior, on the grounds that they were "repressive." The revolutionaries preached that if only people were allowed to "do their own thing" instead of following common social conventions, all men would become brothers in the great "family of man." Life would be hippyishly sweet, gentle, and loving as we all hugged our neighbors and danced around the Maypole.

It didn't work out that way. As our ancestors knew well, people don't naturally behave nicely. In fact, they naturally behave very much like pigs around the trough at feeding time. Manners arose to restrain natural, which is to say utterly self-centered, human behavior. Far from isolating people from one another, manners make normal social intercourse possible. They offer safe, convenient and pleasant ways for strangers to meet, for families to maintain harmonious relations, for offices to be both efficient and nice places to work. They make life easier, not harder.

Consider this vignette from Mrs. Oliver Harriman's *Book of Etiquette*, published in 1942:

> I remember a prominent woman's saying to me once, 'Oh, how much pleasure I get out of remembering the breakfasts of my childhood! There was a rule that all members of the family had to come to the table. We had to be neat. We greeted our parents and each other. We were allowed to take part in the conversation and express our opinions. We never thought of complaining about the food, and of course a cross word or look was out of the question. If such a thing happened, it was flatly declared that

we were ill and could be excused from the table. Everything looked so pretty, too—the colored china, the shining silver, and always a little flower. Because Mother said pretty surroundings made a great difference in how we faced the day. It was like starting out in the morning with everything rosy and beautiful. And if ever any of us had to miss breakfast, if we were really ill, we felt cheated. On Sunday mornings, there was the nice custom of letting each child have a favorite breakfast dish. All through my life I think of my father and mother and brothers and sisters sitting around a table, eating and laughing and talking.'

Rules, the rules we call manners, made that breakfast table possible. Compare that memory with meals in a mannerless modern household, and you will see why so many people are attracted to Retro-manners.

THE GOLDEN RULE

What are Retro-manners? We do not propose to write another book on etiquette; there are plenty of good ones available, new and old. But it may be helpful to consider some general points about manners and the whys and hows of reviving them.

The basis of good manners is the Golden Rule: do unto others as you would have them do unto you. Mrs. Harriman writes, "All people with kindly instincts have inherent good manners." In turn, a person with base instincts, no matter how smooth, is a cad.

The purpose of etiquette is to apply the Golden Rule to everyday situations. Sometimes, admittedly, it can be hard to see the relationship between the principle, consideration for others, and the application, say, eating ice cream with a fork (yes, there are such things as ice cream forks). But an indirect connection is there. In Mrs. Harriman's apt phase, the purpose of the rule is "to smooth social machinery." Just as learning a foreign language makes communication with those who speak it easier, so learning the language of etiquette makes social situations more relaxed and enjoyable. If everyone knows which fork to use, how to make a proper introduction, what to wear to a daytime wedding and the like, a common ground is established on which everyone can meet comfortably. And that is itself a kindness to others.

In contrast, the person who rejects manners usually ends up imposing on others. Often, he justifies himself by saying, "I just want to be me." But when "just being me" includes slurping his soup, ignoring the guest on his right to lecture the guest on his left, not writing a "bread and butter" letter after he has been a houseguest or coming late to a dinner party, he is violating the Golden Rule. When others do the same to him, he is not amused.

Manners, then, are grease for the gears of human interchange. Like grease for mechanical gears, they promote smooth running, reduce friction, and help all parts to work together without stress and strain. So, get yourself a good etiquette book, and take your manners Retro. Do it not for yourself, but as a service to those around you.

MUST WE THEN ACT "HOITY-TOITY?"

Quite the contrary. Miss Manners herself, aka Judith Martin, puts that thought quickly to rest in her excellent "Guide for the Turn-of-the-Millennium" where she notes that "hoity-toitiness should be recognized as the irritant it is." The hoity-toity are putting on an act, and people with manners do not do that. They are genuine. They relate openly and honestly, without any pretense or false airs, to everyone they meet, from the Duke of Omnium to the garbage collector. Traditionally, a gentleman or a lady knew how to talk to people of every rank and station in a way that made them feel comfortable. Hoity-toitiness was the mark of the parvenu, the little shopkeeper recently jumped up from the working class, Molieres' *Bourgeois Gentlehomme*. It earned then, and deserves from Retro-people today, an amused contempt. The real opposite of hoity-toitiness, and an essential ingredient of Retro-manners, is good taste. The very Retro Mrs. Harriman writes:

A fundamental rule of good taste is simplicity. Direct speech, plain dress and simple living are all forms of good taste. Understatement is better than overstatement. … A woman of taste won't do anything that is exaggerated. She won't speak too loudly, won't exaggerate in her talk, and will never overdress. And she will never 'put on airs,' which is what being hoity-toity amounts to. Any affectation of superiority is bad manners; indeed, so is any affectation, period! A person with good manners is marked by a desire to make the other person comfortable, not to appear superior. One of this century's great gentlemen, King Edward VII of England, once had the King of Siam as his guest at a state dinner in Windsor Castle. When the asparagus was served, the King of Siam, who was unfamiliar with all the rules of Western table manners, proceeded to eat it with his fingers. So, promptly, did King Edward (who thereby established a new rule of etiquette: you too may now properly eat asparagus with your fingers).

WHERE DO RETRO-MANNERS APPLY?

They apply to far more than simply what fork to use for oysters (an oyster fork) and where it goes at a place setting (on the right). Mrs. Harriman includes under etiquette rules the quality of speech ("The speaking voice is our visiting card"), the art of conversation, being a homemaker ("In recent years, chiefly because they were too busy earning a living, women haven't done much housekeeping." Perhaps 1942 was not as different from 2018 as we think!), table decorations, good taste ("Good taste is kindness or judgment or sophistication reduced to an instinct. It has to be trained first, but it isn't taste until it becomes an instinct"), the etiquette of bridge and other games, the good sport, on being a good neighbor ("We should never entrust the family skeleton to our neighbor unless we want it exhibited on the back fence"), manners on the job and even on the road ("Of course it goes without saying that nobody should drive a car after drinking even so much as a couple of glasses of beer"). Judith Martin, our modern Miss Manners, illustrates the broad range of etiquette in a short disquisition on "The Meaningless Exchange." She writes:

> Anyone can have a meaningful exchange. Tiresome people do it all the time, long past their and everybody else's bedtime. ... Meaningless exchanges, which are actually more comforting, are the little pleasant phrases one uses to greet or take leave of people, to signify a desire to converse, or simply to be agreeable.

Visitors to France often remark on how pleasantly the French interact (we are not speaking of head waiters and Americans) through their many meaningless exchanges. One goes into a shop, and has a nice exchange of courtesies before getting down to business: no mere "May I help you?" or "Next!" here. In Arab countries, the meaningless exchanges are still more developed: the shopkeeper asks about the well-being of your family and you his, you discuss the weather a bit, often he even offers tea or strong, sweet Turkish coffee long before any business comes up. To do otherwise is looked upon as rude. It may not be a terribly efficient use of time, but it makes both your day and his go more pleasantly. And that is what etiquette is intended to do.

In the wide range of areas they cover, Mrs. Harriman, Miss Manners and the many other writers on etiquette and manners all make the same point: manners apply wherever people interact. And wherever you, as a champion of Retroculture, allow the gentle rules of etiquette to operate, you will find that the interaction goes more smoothly, more pleasantly for all concerned.

ARE RETRO-MANNERS JUST "VICTORIAN"?

No. Though the Victorians generally had good manners (good enough to put up with the many Victorian eccentrics who had bad manners), etiquette and manners go back far beyond the Victorians. Some common rules of etiquette go back to the age of chivalry, when life was sufficiently rough that etiquette helped keep people from hewing at each other with broadswords over minor misunderstandings (by shaking hands, you showed that your right hand did not conceal a dagger). Some etiquette from pre-Victorian times is now proving useful again. In answer to the query, "How does a comfortably married person go about making friends (I mean what I say: friends) with an attractive member of the opposite sex?," Miss Manners replies, "Of course, there are proper ways for ladies and gentlemen to have innocent and rewarding friendships. Such friendships went on quite naturally in the eighteenth century (along with other interesting relationships) before the days when attempting a harmless friendship became simply not worth the scandal."

If your favorite Retroculture era is other than the Victorian, you will find it has its own etiquette, which you may revive. It was not until the mid-1960s that manners as a whole were thrown overboard.

DIFFERENCE WITHOUT DISRESPECT

You may hear some people argue against etiquette. Usually, they say something like, "Oh, manners and etiquette were fine back then, when people were more alike. But nowadays, we're much too diverse for any rules like that. People today come from different ethnic backgrounds, they have different views on almost everything, they may be feminists or conservatives or gay rights people or who knows what. We are just too different now to agree on any rules of conduct."

Well, it is certainly true that people are more open about their differences than they used to be. But does that suggest a lesser or a greater need for manners, politeness, and etiquette? What we need, it would seem, are Retro-manners that allow us to be different without offending others, without showing or causing disrespect, without stuffing our difference in other people's faces to the point where they have to react to it — and then complaining if their reaction is not what we wanted.

One of the Victorians' general rules of etiquette was, "Don't frighten the horses." By that they meant that if you do differ from general norms in some aspect of the way you live, don't thrust it in people's faces. Be sufficiently discreet that other people may politely ignore the difference if they choose to, treating you as if they simply didn't know. Indeed, good manners dictate that they pass over such differences as might disturb them, just as they dictate that you allow them to do so. This permits everyone to get along together quite nicely, which is just what etiquette is intended to do.

The rule, "In bounds, not in your face," is a starting point for Retro-manners among people who differ. But it is not all that old-fashioned etiquette offers to help people who differ get along. If, for example, Ms. Braburner and General Pigge end up at the same dinner party, they can manage quite nicely so long as they demonstrate good manners. They are introduced, and have a polite meaningless exchange: "How do you do?" and "How do you do?" It is time to be seated: The General holds Ms. Braburner's chair, and she smiles and says "Thank you" as she sits down. They restrict their table conversation to what they can discuss pleasantly. As Mrs. Harriman writes, "one should avoid discussion of operations, religion and politics — especially present-day politics — unless one wants the entire party to wind up in the police station." Through it all, General Pigge is imagining himself as Emperor at the coliseum, grinning as he orders the lions let loose on Ms. Braburner, and she is envisioning him served as the main course, trussed, nicely browned, with an apple in his mouth. But by deferring not to each other so much as to the rules etiquette lays down for all, they, and the rest of the company, enjoy their dinner.

Unlike the law, etiquette respects the notion of "separate but equal." Men and women deserve equally polite treatment, but not the same treatment. In social situations (business etiquette is different) the gentleman still holds the door for the lady, he still pulls out her chair at the dinner table, and she still lets him lead when they dance. In fact, Retro-manners between men and women in social situations are very much like dancing (real dancing, not that stuff where people just get out there and shake). It takes two people's combined efforts to make it work. It requires a man who wishes to please, and a woman who wishes to be pleased.

A man who wishes to please is deferential and respectful toward women. No gentleman ever harasses a lady. Indeed, no gentleman tolerates another man doing so. It is barbaric, and in the happy days of yore, the offender could expect to be horsewhipped. The rules of etiquette that apply to relations between men and women embody the deference a man should always show. That is why it is helpful to know them.

Similarly, a lady is gracious in her reception of a gentleman's deference. She allows him to perform the functions properly reserved to the man; as the title of one book says, "real women don't pump gas" (at least when a man is with them). She shows him that she is pleased and grateful. And she looks for proper ways to return his favors, perhaps by introducing into the conversation a topic on which she knows he will shine, or letting him know that the gravlax on the buffet is particularly delicious and should not be missed.

These Retro-rules are by no means hopelessly antique. Miss Manners, who describes herself as an ardent feminist, writes, "Are you ready yet to acknowledge that there are differences between ladies and gentleman?" She lists a number she regards as quite up to date:

> Ladies properly applaud differently from gentlemen. While a gentleman bangs his vertically held palms together in front of him, a lady claps by holding her left palm upward without moving it, and hitting it with downward strokes by her right palm.
>
> When wearing skirts, ladies sit differently from gentlemen. ... Gentlemen either keep both feet on the floor, with the legs slightly parted, or less formally, put the right ankle on the left knee. Females who are not ladies cross their knees. Ladies cross their ankles, keeping the knees together. This is actually very comfortable when you get used to it.
>
> Ladies do not put their names above their return addresses in social correspondence. Ladies do not pour their own wine when gentlemen are present.
>
> Ladies go first through doors but last down steps.
>
> Ladies who are escorted by gentlemen begin carrying packages only when the gentlemen are fully loaded, so to speak.

Ladies wear hats (except in their own houses) as a token of respect.

When they are walking outdoors, American ladies take the side away from the curb. Neither these nor any other rules of etiquette imply inequality between men and women; they simply acknowledge difference.

PUBLIC MANNERS

Public manners are the manners we show to complete strangers, the people we sit next to on the trolley, pass on the street, serve or are served by in shops. Here good manners have almost vanished. The person next to you on the streetcar makes the toilette she should have completed at home or keeps the volume on his headphones so high that you must endure his wretched taste in music. The person passing you on the street is wearing no shirt, confronting you inescapably with the fact that the unclothed human body is as attractive as a plucked chicken. In the shop, the sales people are too busy talking on their cellphones to serve you, or the customer's first words to the clerk are given with a snarl.

How nice it is to live in a truly civil society! Those Americans who have visited such places, in Europe or Asia, find returning home something of a letdown. But America used to be noted for its civility, not that many years ago. It was widely accepted that public manners were a reflection on a person's family; to behave rudely in public was to announce that one had been born in a barroom and reared in a stable. Mrs. Harrison writes, "Whatever we do in public is a reflection of our home environment. If we have consideration for others, we prove ourselves not only good citizens, but members of a good family."

How can Retro-manners begin to return some civility to public life? We should start by looking at our own behavior. In dealing with people we do not know, do we remember the Golden Rule? Nowhere is it easier to ignore than when dealing with strangers, yet nowhere is it more necessary. Do our habits offend others? Would we be offended if someone else did what we ourselves commonly do? Etiquette is a bit like Lent: it causes us to reflect, perhaps somewhat painfully, on ourselves.

Once we have attempted to put our own house in order, it is appropriate we begin to demand some adherence to standards from those around us. We should not tolerate the intolerable, if only because we should speak up on behalf of others. When the scummy kid on the subway has the volume on his headphones cranked way up, it is our duty, not just our right, to tell him (politely) to turn it down. When someone boards an airplane without a shirt of any sort (yes, it happens, usually in California), it is appropriate to express our disapproval. When someone throws his newspaper on the sidewalk, it is entirely proper for us to suggest he pick it up. The modern notion that any expression of disapproval is "intolerant" is wrong; after all, if tolerance were the highest virtue, it would be impossible to oppose evil of any sort. It is the duty of every good citizen to see that certain basic standards of public behavior are maintained, and that when they are violated, there is social sanction in the form of open disapproval. It is all that stands between us and the monkey cage at the zoo.

It is also appropriate for us to take our business to shops that offer polite service, and to shun those that do not. If more of us did that, service would quickly become more mannerly, because the establishments that practice rudeness would go out of business. Civil service is real service. This applies doubly to government agencies that deal with the public; there is nothing quite so rude as rudeness or neglect from people whose salaries are paid by your taxes. Though people with good manners generally avoid creating a scene, a bit of righteous wrath is in order when "public servants" behave like the public's masters.

One particularly hideous custom of modern service people deserves immediate, if polite, rebuke: calling customers by their first names. Such familiarity is rightly reserved to family and friends, not waiters and clerks. From the shopkeeper's standpoint, a bit of formality is good business. People, and not only Retro-people, like being treated respectfully. No one will be offended by being addressed as sir or ma'am (the latter, after all, is how one addresses the Queen of England), or as Mr. or Mrs. or Miss so-and-so when a name is required. Perhaps we should all resolve to let the tip show our feelings the next time the waitress addresses us as "Bill" or "Janie," because she hears us use those names in our own (properly private) table talk.

Even Retrocultural people sometimes make mistakes. Good public manners dictate a quick and sincere apology. (The same is of course true in dealing with people we know; love does not mean never having to say you're sorry!). Similarly, etiquette dictates that if we are the one in whose soup someone else's champagne cork lands, we accept the apology (and the new bowl of soup that should accompany it). Apologies offered and accepted do a great deal to make life run more smoothly and keep everyone's stress level down.

Another rule of public Retro-manners is that noise is not nice. People whose car radios blast into the neighborhoods they drive through, who equip their autos or motorcycles with mufflers that don't muffle, who blast music out of their homes or stores, or who have loud outdoor parties that last well into the night are being very impolite. The rest of us, who have to hold our ears under the bombardment, should not suffer in silence. If the noise is in the neighborhood, it is appropriate to call the offender and suggest he modify his behavior. In the case of noisy vehicles, it is not too much to shake one's umbrella angrily as the offender drives by. Of course, no one with half-decent manners would ever wittingly inflict his preferred noise on others. People with culture instinctively know this; it is never Bach or Mozart one hears blasting from a passing car.

It is time we all joined in collective action to restore the notion of public etiquette. There was a day when good public manners were enforced quite strictly; a gentleman who appeared on the streets in evening dress before 6 o'clock was likely to be hissed by passersby. Perhaps we need not go quite that Retro, but Retroculture can do a great service by making atrocious public manners subject to public censure. Such censure is not rude (and should be expressed politely in all but the most egregious and obviously intentional cases). It is our civic duty.

OFFICE ETIQUETTE

Retro-manners accept the idea that office etiquette and social etiquette are different. For example, on a social occasion, a Retro-gentleman should pick up the check for dinner unless there has been an explicit arrangement beforehand to do otherwise. At a business lunch, it is appropriate for a man and a woman to split the check, or for the woman to pay if the lunch were at her request.

But the fact that social and business etiquette differ does not mean manners cease to apply in the business world. Judith Martin notes, "Miss Manners sees great progress in the fact that ladies and gentlemen can pursue many different occupations, not just the traditional ones of exploiting serfs and marrying money, but it dismays her that they have forgotten how to act like ladies and gentlemen." An article in *The New York Times* noted how prevalent bad manners in the office have become:

> Among the most commonly voiced gripes about both managers and employees were these: starting the day with a request (or a demand) rather than with a good morning, viewing an open door as an invitation to walk in and sit down, routinely leaving desks or offices without informing anyone of whereabouts, dropping trash on the floor and leaving it for the maintenance crew to clean it up and believing that paychecks are compensation enough and that there is no need for pleases and thank-yous for jobs done or service requested.

In 1983, upon releasing his book *The New Office Etiquette* (Poseidon Press), George Mazzei said: "There has been a breakdown in business manners and people are realizing they can no longer deal with the constant rudeness which became a part of the business world when crude young people became superstars."

Smart businesses know that etiquette helps an office run more smoothly, which means greater efficiency. It also raises office morale, which benefits productivity. It is not accidental that Japanese corporations lay great weight on proper office etiquette; on entering a company, a Japanese employee is often given a lengthy manual on the company's rules of etiquette. Several books are available on proper office manners, including George Mazzei's, noted above, and Letitia Baldridge's *Complete Guide to Executive Manners* (Rawson Associates, 1985). An office might do more to improve its competitiveness by investing some tens of dollars in a few copies of these than thousands of dollars in additional computers.

WHICH RETRO-MANNERS?

So far have manners disappeared that just having manners makes you Retro; in fact, it is Retro just to try to have good manners. Fortunately, as the poll quoted at the beginning of this chapter shows, manners are an area where a great many people want to go Retro. The rudeness that has become common in both public and private behavior over the last thirty years turns most people off. And the only solution is to go back to manners and etiquette. Retroculture rules!

But those who want to go Retro with their manners do have a choice to make. You can go with either "updated" etiquette, or revive period etiquette straight.

Miss Manners represents updated etiquette. She writes,

> It is true that some things have changed since Miss Manners and Queen Victoria went to school together: Most adults are in the work force, which means that ladies must practice, and must be treated with, good business manners. ... New customs much be developed for managing the domestic, social, and community realms that ladies used to run. ... Divorce is widespread. ... Servants have been largely replaced by household equipment. ... Weddings are held at what we shall ever so gently call a later state of courtship. ... Society has learned to recognize social units short of marriage and needs rules for dealing with them.

Updated etiquette is perhaps the most practical. It provides rules for situations that did not used to exist (or at least were not recognized by polite people and so needed no etiquette). It is adapted to facts like life without servants and fraternity parties without chaperons. In the main, it is not all that different from the etiquette grandmother used to follow. Most changes are simply adaptations. Writing of etiquette for such modern conveniences such as answering machines, beepers and faxes, Miss Manners notes, "There is some new stuff around since the Etiquette Council held its last congress, some time after the Congress of Vienna. ... You will forgive Miss Manners for speaking of it in old-fashioned terms. The fact is that while ways of doing things may be new, things to be done are generally not, and adaptation, rather than invention, is usually what is needed to cope."

The other option is to go Retro all the way and use the etiquette from "your" era straight. This is more feasible than it might seem (unless your era is the Middle Ages or Augustan Rome). Miss Manners, modernizer though she is, recognizes how much old-fashioned etiquette may still be applied:

> It was on a crumbling page of a hundred-year-old etiquette book that Miss Manners came across the solution to that enduring problem of what to say when confronted with a person whose name you know you are expected to know but don't. The answer comes to us from an anonymous Victorian, apparently a Hero of Etiquette, but described merely as 'a good-natured eccentric.' Beaming a jovial smile at a vaguely familiar face, he would inquire in a pleasant, oh-by-the-way tone, 'You don't happen to remember your name, do you?' Miss Manners is given to perusing aged volumes for just such forgotten devices to ease the difficulties of life. ... Vintage etiquette holds up remarkably well. The human body may have changed, as anyone trying to squeeze into vintage clothing may discover, but the situations into which it manages to get itself are not all that different.

If you take a look through a vintage etiquette book such as Mrs. Harriman's, you will quickly see how much does still apply. For example, writing in the early 1940s, she had this to say on business etiquette:

> Women in business should try to meet men on equal terms without making them overly conscious of the fact that they belong to the opposite sex. And women shouldn't expect any special consideration simply because of their sex. Imagine how much would be accomplished if a man stood up every time his secretary entered the office! The exceptional women who have forged ahead in their fields in spite of all opposition (yes, there is still discrimination against women in business, make no mistake about that) are invariably attractive and feminine. They dress very well and their grooming is always meticulous. But they have a certain impersonal attitude toward their work which makes men forget they are women. They put their work before everything else, in which respect they are akin to men and, therefore, equally successful.

A modern writer might phrase that a bit differently, but the sentiments expressed are unexceptionable, even today. If you adopt period etiquette, there may be some modern situations for which you are not fully prepared, and you may find people thinking your manners a trifle quaint on some occasions. But you can manage the former quite nicely simply by being tactful, and in the latter case, people are more likely to be charmed than offended. Remember, Retroculture is increasingly fashionable, so when you do or say something old-fashioned, people are more likely to envy or emulate you than to take exception.

Whether you choose to update your manners or not, you will have no trouble finding materials to advise you on etiquette. Current books on etiquette are plentiful (we will confess to preferring Miss Manners,' perhaps because even when her advice is up-to-date, her style is pleasantly antique). For older etiquette books, just visit a good used bookstore: they usually have at least a few in stock.

And, of course, you can always just ask your Grandmother.

CHAPTER IX

∽

Retro-Travel

IN RECENT YEARS, travel, as our grandparents and great-grandparents knew it, has almost disappeared. Its sorry replacement is "transportation:" getting from point A to point B as quickly as possible, never mind how miserable the journey. So, we wedge ourselves into tiny airplanes seats, stuffed three to a row, while we pass far over what might be the most glorious scenery on earth. Or we speed along the Interstate highway, our eyes fixed in terror on the truck radiator that fills our rear-view mirror, while the road does its utmost to pass around any local points of interest — not that we could stop for them anyway ("No Stopping on Shoulder, Next Exit 13 Miles"). We tunnel under or speed quickly above America's great rivers, missing their scenic wonders (the Hudson valley is our Rhine). Getting about locally, at least in our cities, has become sheer hell thanks to gridlock, permanent rush hour and a seeming propensity of any truck that carries hazardous waste to find the local beltway and roll over on it. "Getting there is half the fun"? Not anymore.

Well, you know, once upon a time, getting there *was* half the fun. People weren't just "transported," like so many sides of mutton. They travelled. They travelled in style, they travelled in ways that allowed them to appreciate the places they passed through, and, incredible as it may sound to us, they travelled for pleasure. Then, as now, travel had certain inconveniences — the snowy white linen in the Pullman berth was, come morning, grey from locomotive soot — but journeys were events, experiences, even adventures, filled with new sights, sounds and people, memorable quite apart from where they ended up. Edna St. Vincent Millay wrote, "There isn't a train I wouldn't take, no matter where it is going." What early 21st century poet would write that about seat 9E (center) on the 12:30 PM flight out of La Guardia for LAX?

Retro-travel aims at recovering the pleasure of the journey itself. Sometimes, as when on vacation, this requires little more than a decision to take some extra time along the way. In other cases, it may take some imagination. Business travel (now almost all just "transportation") is a case in point. What business would allow its employees to enjoy travel on business? Well, perhaps one that thought a bit. Not only can real travel sometimes save a company money (taking a train between, say, Washington and Boston, is cheaper), it may also raise the efficiency of employees. Is a company best served by representatives who come into a key meeting exhausted, their body clocks gone haywire from too many time zones crossed too quickly, their brains addled and their nerves frazzled? Or would the "big deal" best be clinched by someone who had been given more time away from the office for a while, with a chance to think and reflect? More and more companies are discovering that the straight line between two points is not necessarily the best route if you want good performance from your people. A well-traveled representative, not one who has just undergone the shock of being packaged and shipped, may bring home the biggest dividends.

Similarly, local travel is often possible, despite gridlock. Often, the key is simply leaving the car at home. "Public transit" may bring to mind crowded buses and grimy subways, but in a growing number of cities, modern rail systems offer relaxed, pleasant ways to travel. And when you get off, you can get your daily exercise and see a bit of the town by walking to your destination. That is how most people got around in the years up until the 1940s, when, in a sad mistake, most cities got rid of their streetcars (like the famous "Red Cars" in

Los Angeles). You can read your paper on the train, or just gaze at the passing scene, unworried about traffic jams and overturned trucks, then perhaps make a quick stop at the bakery on your walk to the office. You arrive relaxed, at peace with the world, and with a few new ideas about the day's work from the unhurried, unharried time you had to think on the train.

Perhaps the key to really traveling, from place to place or just in town, is simply to start doing it. Like much of Retroculture, it begins with your decision: to start to enjoy the trip itself, instead of just focusing on "getting there." As the saying goes, take some time to smell the flowers. Think about how you might go a new way, or travel by a different mode, so as to get something out of the journey. As the rest of this chapter points out, there are a number of different ways to travel, and they all offer something more than "transportation."

THE TRAIN

If God had meant for man to fly, He would never have given us the railways. The airplane gets you there (most of the time, anyway), but that's about all that can be said for it. The train, in contrast, is Retro-travel. If offers many of the things people pay lots of money for when they go on cruises, and unlike a cruise, it still takes you someplace.

"Dinner in the diner, nothing could be finer," is a line from the famous song, "Chattanooga Choo-choo." And it's true. Where else can you enjoy a freshly prepared dinner while the countryside goes whizzing by in a grand show? No plane or car or bus can offer that. Nor can they offer a private room each night, with your very own bed; but a railway sleeping car can, and does. Even in humble coach class, trains offer space and comfort greater than most airlines manage in first class.

Unlike the plane or the car, the train is social. You don't just meet the people who sit near you. You wander about in a train, meeting whomever you like. The lounge car is a "common room," where it is easy to strike up a conversation. In the diner, tables are shared; you may sit with, say, a grandmother from Dakota's farm country on her way to visit her grandchildren, an architecture student returning home for vacation, and a businessman whose company knows the night train saves "real" time — and money.

If you prefer solitude, you can usually find that, too, in a seat by yourself or a compartment (called a "roomette," and a remarkable tribute to efficient use of space) in a sleeper. There, you can enjoy a panorama nothing else can offer, as the train, unencumbered by roadside shopping centers and Vegas' strips, cuts its straight and narrow way through America. Up the Hudson valley, through the Pennsylvania hills, across the great plains and among the Rocky Mountains, the train gives you our nation, displayed at its finest right in front of your nose. You have nothing to do but relax, in the cushioned comfort of the safest form of travel, and enjoy it.

Until about seventy-five years ago, most people travelled by train. And most of them enjoyed it. On the whole, the trains then were better than those we have today. But Amtrak, after some early years plagued by worn-out cars and surly employees, now does a decent job. The Western trains have splendid equipment, double-decker cars where you ride high above the rails on a smooth, silent magic carpet. And they have a pleasant Retro feel to them, suggesting the great days of the Super Chief and San Francisco Zephyr. While Amtrak doesn't yet offer the ambiance of the 20th Century Limited, it does provide something very like the train travel experience our grandparents and great-grandparents knew. It isn't just transportation; it is travel — Retro-travel.

It is also increasingly popular. More and more people are discovering the pleasures of Retro-travel with Amtrak, with the result that it can be hard to get tickets, especially in the summer. Sleeping car space is often sold out months in advance on the Western trains. But prices are moderate, and Amtrak now serves 500 towns and cities. You can probably take the train on your next trip, no matter where you're going; just plan ahead. If you haven't done it in years, or perhaps never,

FIGURE 6. The parlor-lounge car of the Great Northern "The International" train. (Source: Wikimedia Commons)

you're in for a treat. You'll find out just how much you've been missing, crammed into seat 9E on the tin bird.

FIRST CLASS "PLUS"

In the great days of the railways, a few trains were truly grand: "First Class Plus," they were called, because they not only required a first class ticket, but a supplementary fare on top of that. Such were the 20th Century Limited,[14] Santa Fe's Deluxe and later its Super Chief, and a few others. The noted rail writer and photographer Lucius Beebe wrote of the 20th Century:

> Placed in service in 1902 as an all-Pullman, extra fare, *de luxe* conveyance for the affluent and the powerful of a well-ordered world, it became the

---

14 An express passenger train on the New York Central railroad. — Editor.

stuff of folklore, the central theme of plays and motion pictures and possessed of perhaps the most ample biography of any train in the record of surface transportation. Great drama and momentous decisions of state and finance rode its luxuriously upholstered cars and it was and is the only train to arouse so fierce and enduring a loyalty that a club of gentlemen was organized for the sole purpose of riding aboard it and holding their annual dinner *en route*.

"First Class Plus" is now also making a comeback, and in a few places, you may now travel as the *élite et bon ton* of the early years of this century did. A touch of "first class plus" may be found on one of Amtrak's most unusual trains: Autotrain. Autotrain carries people with their automobiles from Lorton, Virginia to Florida, saving them a dreary drive on the Interstate. For those who take it first class, in a sleeping car, Amtrak has created something of the feel of the great trains. Not only is the service excellent, but the separate first-class-only dining car is a dome car. You ride high above the rest of the train under a great glass bubble, enjoying first-rate cuisine elegantly served, dining literally under the stars.

Quite separate from Amtrak is another bit of Retro-travel, in this case a true rail cruise: the dinner train. Dinner trains don't really go anywhere; you get off where you got on. But in the meantime, you have taken a leisurely train ride through the countryside while enjoying dinner in the diner. The food ranges from home style to gourmet dining, but in each case, you get to experience that unique attribute of rail travel, the ability to dine while on the move. Dinner trains may now be found in many locations throughout the country, and they are an excellent way to introduce yourself to the Retro-pleasure of riding the rails.

Amtrak's trains and most dinner trains are pulled by electric or diesel locomotives. Except to rail fans, they aren't very interesting—just big boxes than hum. In the great days of railway travel, most of the engines were steam. A steam engine, more than any other of man's contrivances, is alive. It hisses, it breathes, it exhibits all its workings to the observing eye. Fortunately, Retroculture already includes a revival of steam locomotives, for special trips. Some are run by railroads, such as Norfolk Southern. Others are owned and run by museums and clubs of steam fans. All offer splendid Retro travel, usually in the summer months, and often with antique passenger cars to complement the old-fashioned locomotives. On these trips, you can really get a feel for what train travel used to be like, right down to the occasional cinder in your eye. For the Retro person, nothing is quite equal to travel behind steam, with its unforgettable sights and sounds, and in them the history of the technology that, more than any other, knitted this country together and made of us a nation.

Special trips and steam runs by museums can now be found in most parts of the country. Call or write your nearest railway museum, or contact your local chapter of the National Rail Historical Society. Trips range from runs of an hour or so over a few miles of museum-owned track to excursions of several days covering a thousand miles of main-line railroad. Many special trips offer limited, extra-fare first class accommodations; often, the First Class cars are Pullmans or parlor cars from the teens or 20s. For those looking for Retro-travel, the extra fare is worth it.

However you choose to do it, sometime, somewhere, take a train ride. Trains aren't just part of the Retro life; they are an essential element, because they are how most of our forefathers travelled most of the time. To understand how they saw the world and gain a feeling for their lives, we all need to ride a train at least once. Chances are, if you do it once, you'll get hooked. You will find just how nice real travel — train travel — can be.

URBAN TRAVEL: THE SECOND COMING OF THE TROLLEY CAR

In 1888, the first practical, successful electric streetcar system began operation in Richmond, Virginia. Within a decade, trolley systems were proliferating wildly all across the nation. Just as our ancestors got around the country on the train, they got around town on the streetcar.

But by the 1920s Henry Ford's Model T was rolling off the assembly lines in the millions, and soon people were leaving trolley cars for private automobiles. By the 1930s, trolley systems were being abandoned right and left, with buses taking over the remaining riders of public transit. The few systems that survived World War II (when ridership boomed, thanks to gas rationing) were almost all closed soon thereafter.

The rise and fall of the electric streetcar was rapid — it was the most ephemeral of all capital-intensive industries — but also typical. One technology was replaced by another. But starting in the 1980s, something very untypical happened: using essentially the same technology, the streetcar began a comeback. Sometimes under the fancy new name of "Light Rail," streetcar systems were opened in a number of cities, beginning in 1981 with San Diego. Now, new trolleys are running in Portland, Oregon; Sacramento; San Jose; Los Angeles; Buffalo; Kansas City; Cincinnati; Edmonton and Calgary, Canada; and in a few cities that had the wisdom never entirely to get rid of them, including San Francisco, New Orleans, Philadelphia and Boston. Like Lazarus, our old friend from Toonerville has risen from the dead!

The return of the streetcar offers Americans in a growing number of cities the opportunity for urban Retro-travel. It's Retro because it's the way we use to get to work, go downtown to shop, and visit our friends in town, from the 1890s into the inter-war years. It's travel, and not mere transit, because riding a streetcar is fun! At the height of the first trolley era, early in the century, millions of people took pure trolley joy-rides — riding just for the pleasure of riding. Many of the cars of that era had open sides, and on a warm summer evening, an easy way to enjoy a cooling breeze and just relax was to spend a nickel on a trolley ride, particularly on a line that ran out into the country as many did. There were trolley party-cars, with Victrolas.[15] One young couple even spent their honeymoon taking the trolley from Delaware to Maine, then wrote a book about it! "Ride a Mile and Smile the While" was the trolleys' slogan, and a great many people did exactly that.

Riding the trolley car is still fun today. It feels entirely different from a bus. The seats are wider and more comfortable, with more leg room. There is no vibration from the electric motors. It feels — well, like it's riding on rails, which of course it is. It's smooth and quiet — and non-polluting. You look down the busy street to either side and see into all the shop windows. Then, often, the trolley right-of-way cuts off from the street at the edge of town, and you sail through the countryside, unencumbered by the side-of-the-road detritus of modern life. Unlike the subway, stuck in its dark tube, the trolley usually runs on the surface where there is lots to see and watch. Free from the need to stare into the bumper of the car in front of you, you relax, enjoy — and travel.

In some cities, you can even travel on antique trolley cars, with the polished wood and brushed brass of an earlier and more gracious era. New Orleans' streetcars were built in the 1920s, and, unschlocked by "modernization," they retain the charm of their era as they glide down St. Charles Avenue, past many of America's most stately homes. San Jose has a downtown Trolley Mall where antique cars, some dating to the early years of the century, mix with modern Light Rail Vehicles. San Francisco's Market Street line carries 20,000 people per day on antique streetcars…

The streetcar renaissance is Retroculture at its best; the recovery of an almost-lost way of travel as an antidote to gridlock and automobile exhaust. The next time you're in a city that has trolley cars, take a ride. You'll quickly see why commuting was not, for our grandparents, the

---

15 Victrola was a brand name of phonograph. — Editor.

hassle it has become for us. You can travel — really travel — in the city, thanks to the miracle of 19th-century technology.

> "Believe me, my young friend, there is nothing — absolutely nothing — half so much worth doing as simply messing about in boats."
>
> — WATER RAT, *The Wind in the Willows*

Before the glories of train travel were given to us by the power of steam and steel, the principal mode of travel was by boat. Journeys overland, by horse or carriage, were rough and slow and usually an ordeal. But by water, travel — getting from one place to another enjoyably — was possible. As late as the 1930s, people still travelled by boat on America's inland and coastal waterways. Great sidewheel steamships like the *Seeandbee* (so large that in World War II she was converted, side wheels and all, into an aircraft carrier to train pilots on Lake Michigan) connected the Great Lakes ports on overnight runs, and the Hudson River Day Line still ran through American's most gorgeous gorge with floating palaces like the *Alexander Hamilton*. Up until the early 1960s you could still take the night boat down the Potomac from Washington to Norfolk, your automobile stowed safely on the lower deck.

Today, there are still opportunities to Retro-travel by boat. One kind of boat, ferryboats, are even making something of a comeback. Displaced in recent decades by bridges carrying interstates — mere transportation — the humble but likeable ferries are reappearing, like the trolley car, as a way around the traffic jams all that highway construction engendered. In San Francisco, across Chesapeake Bay to Maryland's eastern shore, and in New York City new ferry services have recently been launched to widespread acclaim: Wrote *The New York Times*:

Long before dawn, commuters arrive at the dock in Weehauken, NJ., first one by one, then in briskly moving masses. Briefcases in hand, they board a blue and white ferry marked 'Midtown.' And for the next five minutes, until the Port Imperial ferry docks at West 38th Street in Manhattan, serenity seems to settle over the crowd.

'Before the overwhelming assault on my senses, I just like to have a few Buddha-like moments,' said one woman who sat on the upper deck, her eyes closed and her face lifted into a breeze rolling off the Hudson River. …

'It's a kind of renaissance,' said David Phraner, a transportation planner for the Port Authority of New York and New Jersey. The idea of ferries crisscrossing New York's rivers like bootlaces is an old idea made new. …

'This is the nicest thing that ever happened to me,' said William Kremer as be boarded a Weehawken Ferry from Manhattan. 'I drove for more than twenty-six years and I'd get stuck for at least forty-five minutes twice a week. My nerves were totally shot.'

Richard Maxwell, an insurance broker who was boarding the afternoon ferry to Highlands, New Jersey, is another convert. 'I used to take the train, then the car, and it was a killer,' he said. 'This is much better. It has changed my life.'

Before the 1960s, when the world went to pot, the grandest boating most travelers enjoyed was "Crossing the Pond" — taking one of the great ocean liners to Europe. Grand hotels afloat, they offered every comfort: *haute cuisine* dining, dancing in the ballroom, swimming pools and movie theaters, even skeet shooting off the fantail. They were the epitome of travel, of pleasure found in the journey itself.

It is an experience the traveler may yet enjoy, thanks to the first and greatest of Great Britain's trans-Atlantic steamship companies, Cunard. Cunard's *Queen Mary* still plies the Atlantic fall through spring, upholding the grand tradition. She is a thoroughly British ship, with afternoon tea and a proper sense of dignity and decorum. Nor is she strictly for the super-rich; regular fares begin at just over $1000, and standby tickets are even less. Make no mistake, crossing the Atlantic on the *Queen Mary*, is not a mere "cruise." You are really going somewhere, either There or Back Again. And you are doing it in style: Retrostyle. You would not be surprised to find a Vanderbilt in the neighboring deck chair, or meet a Windsor over dinner.

If Retro-travel by boat does gain new favor, there is an exciting possibility for resurrecting a mode of travel long gone. What is it? Canals.

In England, for almost fifty years people have been restoring 18th- and early 19th-century canals. There, you can charter your own boat and run it yourself. The boats are patterned after the canal boats of the past, "narrowboats" as the English call them (and theirs are very narrow indeed!). Driven now by a motor instead of pulled by horses, they nonetheless move at the same deliberate speed of a few miles per hour, allowing a leisurely and detailed study of the English countryside. You have on board comfortable bunks and a galley where you may cook. You may stop where you like to explore a town, dine in a local pub, or take a walk cross country. A growing number of Americans now take "canalling" vacations in Great Britain, seeing that country as they might have seen it not just one, but two hundred years ago.

In the east, America also had its canals. The Erie canal still operates, as the modernized New York State Barge Canal. But New England, the Mid-Atlantic states, and even the midwest also had canals, most built in the early 19th century and abandoned early in the 20th. Enough remains of many of them, like the C&O canal that ran from Washington, D.C. to Cumberland, Maryland (now a national park), to permit their restoration. Imagine taking a week-long cruise through the heart of the Allegheny Mountains, among some of America's best scenery, stopping at historic towns like Harper's Ferry and traveling at a pace where you would see as much as if you walked. If it's happened in England, why not here?

MOTORING

Driving isn't traveling. For the most part, it is a chore. In rush hour, or on crowded interstates surrounded by 18-wheelers, it can be a nightmare. The automobile, originally a liberating device, has become confining.

But it need not always be so. Retroculture offers an alternative to driving: motoring. In motoring, the object is to enjoy the journey, to travel, not merely to "get someplace." In the early days of the automobile, if you just wanted to get someplace, you could almost always do so faster on the train or the trolley. You went by motor-car because it was something of an adventure. You could stop along the way to see points of interest, explore a different road or slow down and see the countryside.

Retro-travel by automobile essays to recover the spirit of long-ago motoring. You can do this even on some of your daily rounds, just by taking the old road or the back road instead of the new highway. It takes a bit more time, but provides a break instead of a tension headache. Or, you may choose to plan motoring trips, where the goal from the outset is to take the road less travelled. Either way, you may experience again what the automobile used to provide before there were too many of them.

While you can use any kind of car for motoring, there is one variety particularly suited to it: the open car, roadster or convertible. From the first automobiles through the 1920s, most cars were open. Today, an open car best offers the feel of old-time motoring, of the days of linen dusters and goggles, big hats and veils. You get the sights and sounds and smells of the country much more strongly than if you are sealed up in a steel cocoon, the radio or CD player filling your ears while the climate control system makes summer and winter indistinguishable. Nor is top-down motoring just a summer sport; few motoring pleasures exceed pottering along in an open car on a fall day, a lap robe and the car heat keeping your feet toasty while you enjoy the crisp, clean air. Fortunately, open cars have been an early

Retro-revival. After almost disappearing in the 1970s, they have made a strong comeback. Today, you can find them in almost any size or configuration. You don't have to have one to motor, of course, but they do offer that extra touch of the past Retro-travelers always seek.

Let's say you've equipped yourself with a suitable machine and are set for some serious Retro-motoring. Where might you start? One of the best places is an old map or atlas. Not surprisingly, you are likely to find most of the past along the oldest roads. Sometimes, the old roads have lost their character because too much that is modern has been built up along them; they have become victims of the "Vegas strip." But in a good number of places, time, in the form of superhighways, has bypassed the old roads, leaving them with the feel of days gone by. You go through the towns, not around them, past the farms and country houses (built close to the road in the days before automobiles), along by the rivers and the railways, following what are often the earliest paths the first settlers took. You may stop where you choose (no signs warning "Emergency Stops Only"), slow to read the historical markers, and when you find an especially pretty spot, get out and walk a bit.

You may readily combine such "shunpike" motoring with travel on special "scenic routes." Many maps mark highways with especially nice scenery, or AAA can route you for the best viewing. Often, the old road and the scenic route are one and the same.

The revolt against the plastic, everywhere-the-same chain motels has given us suitable Retro-lodging to accompany motoring, in the growing number of country inns and Bed and Breakfast accommodations. A number of guidebooks list such places, and many local tourist information services can also point you toward them. B&Bs in particular are often quite reasonably priced; even in a tourist area like the Laurel Highlands of Maryland and Pennsylvania, pleasant accommodations can be found for $35 or even $25 per night. In some towns, you may also find survivors from the pre-motel era, in the form of Tourist Homes. These may offer what the Retro-traveler seeks most:

a place to stay that has not changed since the 1930s or even 1920s. In a few places, like Cape May, New Jersey, you may even find one of the great 19th-century summer resort hotels, still open for business and largely or wholly unmodernized. The Hotel Chalfont in Cape May, now designated as a national landmark, still has the original air conditioning (a set of louvered doors on each room, to admit the sea breeze), the original entertainment (wicker rockers on the porch and a library well stocked with third-rate Edwardian novels), and a dining room served by the same family of cooks for generations. Staying there, you half expect to find that your Ford or Mazda has been transmogrified into a Packard or a Hupmobile.[16]

Motoring is also enhanced by finding Retro establishments in which to eat. The small towns through which the old roads pass often hold survivors from the time before the fast food deluge. These tend to be of two types. The first is the local "nice place to have dinner," known generically to our grandparents as the "Green Palm." The menu is strictly American, the waitresses usually grandmotherly, and the prices reasonable. The other type is the lunch counter, known universally (at least in the Northeast) as "Harry the Greek's." A close cousin to the diner, which you may also find on occasion, Harry the Greek's is eggs over easy with real (not frozen) home fries for breakfast, or a grilled cheese and a fountain coke for lunch. Harry is usually a bit of a character and a good guide to the local scene; his prices are downright cheap. Both Harry's and the Green Palm are essentially unchanged since the 1940s.

Needless to say, the Retro-traveler does not eat in fast food joints, those gustatory cesspools of the Interstate Era. Thrown upon his own resources, he would rather stop in the local grocery and obtain the fixings of a picnic. In a number of states, a thoroughly Retro site for picnicking may still be found: the roadside park. Often built by the CCC in the 1930s, the roadside park offers some picnic tables, an

---

16 The Hupmobile was a popular car series built by the Hupp Motor Car Company between 1909 and 1939. — Editor.

outhouse, and a water pump. It also frequently presents a charming face to the old road on which you will find it: a grove of noble trees, a small stream, some well-shaded nooks, even a nice view over the countryside. Once, roadside parks were heavily used; now, bypassed by the Interstates, you are likely to have plenty of privacy. Sadly, some states, such as Ohio, have eliminated their roadside parks for that very reason. But those that survive may take a new lease on life as Retroculture brings a return to genuine motoring.

And if a roadside park is not available, you can almost everywhere find a pleasant alternative: have your picnic in a cemetery. That may seem strange to those accustomed to things modern, but it used to be quite common. The first "garden" cemetery in the nation (as distinguished from the simple churchyard), which opened in Boston in the 19th century, encouraged picnicing from the start (and still does). Cemeteries are quiet, green, and often well sited, and the people there are probably glad of the company. Of course, here as everywhere, Retroculture people are careful to clean up after themselves.

The combination of scenic old roads, small towns and farms, country inns to stay in and Green Palms to dine in can resurrect the automobile from its dreary functionality and make it again what it was in its early days, an amusing toy — especially if it is an open car. But there is one rule you must follow if you wish to attempt motoring: don't plan to go too far too fast. One hundred miles in a day is probably a good point from which to figure. In flat country, with farms and towns far-spaced, you may manage more without descending into mere driving; in the mountains, or in places like New England where an interesting town waits around each corner, you may find you wish to do less. Remember, when you go motoring, your real destination is the road itself. As a Retroculture person, if you wanted to get someplace in a hurry, you'd simply take the train.

WALKING AND BICYCLING

Most people who have adopted a Retroculture lifestyle are looking for a world which, as J.R.R. Tolkien put it, is less noisy and greener. One way to find such a world is to get around quietly, without assistance from noisy motors, by walking or on a bicycle.

As we noted earlier in this volume, our ancestors got a good bit of exercise, though none of them owned Nautilus machines or went jogging.[17] They simply walked to get where they were going. Walking remains the best way to get around if you really want to see where you are. You can explore where you want, stop when you want, and you never go so fast that you are likely to miss something. You will never see a new city or town or bit of country so well as when you walk it. And even in places you know, you will see something different almost every time you go walking. Modern people may object that walking is too slow, but Retroculture seeks to slow life down a bit; it goes quite fast enough without any motorized assistance. And you may speed up your journey by combining walking with use of public transport. If you walk to and from your stop on the trolley or railway line, you get your daily exercise and take a breather from the day's otherwise hectic pace.

As any student of the 1880s or 1890s can tell you, the first revolution in personal mobility — the ability to go where you want without consulting schedules — was not the automobile but the bicycle. By the turn of the century, people were getting around locally quite nicely — and quietly — by bike. In some places, like Holland, they still do.

By the 1950s, bicycles in the United States were largely relegated to children. Fortunately, in the last thirty or so years the bicycle has made a big comeback. Millions of adults now own bicycles, and use them. Many metropolitan areas have extensive networks of bike paths; maps are readily available in map shops or tourist bureaus. A number of rural areas also have bike trails, converted from abandoned railway

---

17 A brand of home fitness machine. — Editor.

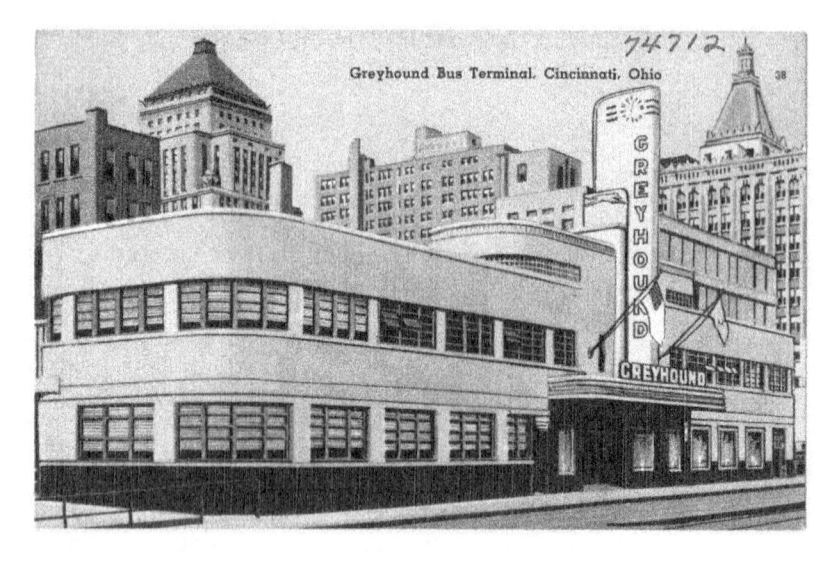

FIGURE 7. Greyhound Bus Terminal, Cincinnati, Ohio. (Source: Boston Public Library)

lines. These make good biking, because grades are gentle (for a railway, a 2% grade is steep). Mountain bikes have opened the door to cross-country bicycling as well, at least for the hardy.

Retroculture takes full advantage of the return of the bicycle, not just by joining in recreational bicycling, but by reintroducing the bicycle as a regular way to get around. The bicycle need not just be a toy; often, it may substitute for the automobile for local travel. And it can make getting around locally really traveling, because on a bicycle you see much more than you do from a car.

A couple modest changes to the average bicycle can help make it a practical and pleasant way to get around. First, put a comfortable seat on it. These are now readily available from most bicycle shops. Second, add a basket, either one up by the handlebars or two over the rear wheels. That way, you can carry a bag of groceries home from the store, or even two. So modified, you may find your bicycle handier in many cases than your car. And, as with walking, you will be getting your exercise naturally, while doing something else. You may not need that health club membership after all.

Retro-travel, like other aspects of Retroculture, turns to the past to find better ways to live in the present. Trains, trolleys, boats, motoring, bicycling and walking were the ways our ancestors got around. They offer ways we can do the same, and with less stress, less pollution, and more of a chance to enjoy the journey itself. We may all have to take that 9E seat in the airplane on occasion, or drive on the Interstate. But we don't have to make either of those the norm. With a bit of foresight, we can plan our travel so it really is travel. And, once again, getting there can be at least half the fun.

CHAPTER X

∽

Retro-Business

President Coolidge said, "The business of America is business." That makes Retroculture good news for America, because Retroculture opens the door to many new business opportunities in both products and services. Just as businesses have always gotten ahead by thinking of something new, now, in the Retroculture era, they can get ahead by thinking of something old.

As we have noted throughout this book, Retroculture people will want to get many of the things they need by making them themselves or by finding the genuine old articles. Retroculture is not one more cry to "Go out there and buy!" But at the same time, they will want old-fashioned versions of the things they need to buy, and also some Retro-services. Meeting those needs offers some interesting, and potentially rewarding, business opportunities. That, in turn, offers Retropeople who are in business a chance to expand their Retroculture world to include their work. What could make work more rewarding for, say, a shop owner whose favorite era is the 1920s than running a shop like one in the 1920s?

Let's take a look at a number of different businesses and see what opportunities Retroculture might offer.

Imagine for a moment that you are a big executive with one of the automobile companies in Detroit. For years, your company has steadily been losing market share to imports. If you try to copy the imports, you find yourself playing a game they know better than you do; their small cars are better than your small cars. If you take a jump ahead of them with a futuristic design, they adjust so quickly and copy you that you get only a brief respite. You keep on asking yourself the question, what can my company build that people will want and that the imports can't simply copy?

How about the 1957 Chevy? Or the 1956 Ford Thunderbird? Or the 1948 Chrysler Imperial?

Retroculture might offer Detroit its desperately needed answer to the import invasion. Wouldn't you like to be able to buy one of America's most famous cars again? Of course, there would have to be some changes under the hood to accommodate the new pollution and safety laws. But why couldn't Detroit make the great old cars again, with those changes? The cars were basically pretty simple, and should not cost a fortune to produce. And how would the imports compete? The 1957 Toyota resembled a motorized chamber pot and would not find many buyers here (in Japan, Japanese car companies have made some new versions of their 1950s cars, and they have sold like sushi). And how could, say, Toyota credibly copy an American car from the past? Volkswagen already has its new Beetle, Britain has given us a new Minim and Fiat offers a new 500, but with those few exceptions Detroit would own the Retro-automobile market. And people would be lined up all the way down the street and around the corner to buy American cars.

In other areas, we see Retroculture already having some effects on business, but we can also identify new Retro-needs that aren't being met. For example, we see a wide variety of reproductions of colonial furniture, and now some Victorian furniture is being reproduced as well. But there are still major market opportunities in Retro-furniture, such as inexpensive "starter" furniture that reflects old styles; sets designed to give a whole room or several rooms the "feel" of a certain period, including appropriate accessories; and reproductions of styles from more recent eras, from the 1930s through the 1950s. Of course, used furniture stores, antique dealers and shops specializing in furniture restoration may find good business in offering furniture from the recent past as well. For young people just starting out, the 1940s or 1950s may be just as attractive as the colonial or Victorian periods and a great deal more affordable.

As we noted earlier, Retro-clothing is a somewhat particularized interest; not everyone who is interested in Retroculture wants to dress Retro. But even so, the Retro-clothing market will expand as Retroculture become more popular. At present, that market is served largely by a few specialized mail order catalogues and by the fact that some "new" fashions harken strongly back to the 1940s and 1950s.

What business opportunities does Retro-clothing offer? As Retroculture grows, the main line catalogues might find good business in offering special Retro sections. Imagine, for example, a special section in the Penny's catalogue that offered selections of clothing from earlier eras. Might not many people want to order one or two things "just for fun," like perhaps a nice sun dress from the 1930s, or a little boy's sailor suit from 1910, or some plus-fours for Dad for the golf course (some golf pros are wearing them again)? Further, stores like Sears might find sufficient demand to support Retro offerings on the store floor, perhaps in a special, easily identified section.

Many people would want to come and browse, just to look at the old styles and enjoy the memories they would bring. And those who come to browse often buy, new styles as well as old. In some areas, particularly those with large tourist populations, there might be enough of a Retro-market to support small shops devoted solely to Retro-clothing, newly made as well as old. After all, some shops that sell old clothing are doing quite nicely; how could it hurt business to offer new clothes as well, made to old patterns?

Many people are looking for some interesting clothes to buy, at a time when everything either looks all the same or like it's made for cabaret performers in Weimar Berlin. By mixing contemporary and historic styles, major merchandisers might be able to give their lines a lift while remaining relevant to middle class, middle age buyers, i.e., most people. We predict some major retailers will try it, and find it works.

Publications are another major market where Retroculture could be good business. Much is already happening here, with magazines (both print and online) like *Victoria, Old House Journal, Chap Magazine, Reminisce,* and the like — and of course with this book. But the demand for Retroculture reading materials is likely to grow faster than it can be met. It will include a demand for books on how to "go Retro" for specific eras; for reproductions of books from earlier eras, especially works on architecture, home decorating, landscaping, entertaining, cooking and the like; and for reproductions of periodicals from the past, especially popular magazines such as *Colliers* and *The Saturday Evening Post.* Those magazines filled the role now largely taken by television, providing entertainment for leisure moments, and with many Retro homes de-emphasizing electrical devices it is a role they can fill again.

Appliances are an area where demand for Retro-styles is likely to be strong. Williams-Sonoma already offers a reproduction of the classic gas stove of the 1920s and 30s, the kind high on legs with the oven beside and above the burners (and with a nice shelf above the burners for warming the plates). Another classic, the 1940s Electrolux vacuum cleaner, is being offered as remanufactured originals. And, of course, 19th-century wood-fired, cast-iron kitchen stoves have made a big comeback.

But think how much more could be done. Many single people don't need large refrigerators; if General Electric were to re-issue its famous "monitor-top" refrigerator from the 1930s, both the size and the style would be perfect for them. It would be easy to make electric mixers, irons, toasters (the old side-openers do need watching, but they are perfect for bagels), waffle irons, indeed almost any appliance to patterns from earlier eras. Sometimes the "guts" might be modernized, and sometimes perhaps best not—the originals were simple and lasted forever.

Appliances, especially those usually left sitting out in the kitchen, lend a touch of authenticity to period settings that nothing else can equal. They re-create Grandma's kitchen, that magical place of memory that means permission for little boys and girls to eat all the things their mothers said weren't good for them. That's the kitchen we Retro-people want in our houses. After all, we still are those boys and girls.

Consumables offer a Retro-market that manufacturers have only begun to touch. Here, Retro-people most often are looking for labels and packaging that recall the past. Some companies have been smart enough to keep their labels unchanged over the years; look at the typeface on a Helman's mayonnaise jar, or the little girl on the label of Morton's salt ("When it rains, it pours.") Several breakfast cereals, including Rice Krispies, have put out boxes with antique labels to mark the anniversary of the cereal's introduction.

But these only point the way to the potential market. Retro-people will want reproduction packaging on a wide variety of products—in fact, on everything where the product itself existed in the past. From soap powder and toothpaste through canned food and packaged bread, revival of historic labels and slogans (or both combined, as was brilliantly done by "Uneeda Biscuit") is possible. And wherever it is possible, it will be wanted. Through Retroculture, people are seeking to give their homes the look and feel of a past era. In that attempt, details like the appearance of the cleanser bottle by the sink or the cans in the kitchen cupboard are very helpful. They can make the difference between a place that looks like it is trying to feel like the past, and one that really does feel that way. And—an important consideration—it is a very inexpensive way to get the desired effect. Products with historic labels need not—and where they have been manufactured, do not—cost any more than those with modern labels.

There is also a growing Retro-market for consumables and other small items that have disappeared over the years. The Vermont

Country Store catalogue offers such items as a bread box, sleeve garters, rubber swim shower caps, Panama hats, Florida water, and Lydia Pinkham Herbal Compound. That market will expand as Retroculture spreads, and who can say where its upper limit might be? We might yet see the return of the Packard automobile—or, in keeping with concern for the environment, the Baker Electric.

People not only want to buy Retro-products; they would like to buy them in Retro-stores. Merchandising can find potential new markets through Retroculture. We are seeing a bit of that already in the return of the ice cream parlor and, in a few places, the milkman. What about the return of the great department stores of the 1920s and 1930s? A few still survive, though as shadows of what they were. Perhaps they could lead the revival of their breed. They were wonderful places to shop, with all the variety a mall offers but greater convenience, consistently knowledgeable service people, beautiful displays (especially around the holidays; what boy who grew up back then does not remember the elaborate model train layouts in the department stores at Christmas?), and often a quiet and genteel restaurant where shoppers could find an excellent lunch at a reasonable price.

There are other possibilities for Retro-stores. As architects such as Andres Duany and Elizabeth Plater-Zyberk recreate genuine communities, the corner store might make a comeback—the little place, often just a room in someone's home, that sold bread, milk, and pipe tobacco to people who lived within walking distance. The country store that sells local products, like the wonderful Amish butter and cheese you can find in Ohio, Maryland and Pennsylvania, might start to spread again. Instead of supermarkets, we might again find small shops specializing in meat or fish or cheese or produce, such as you still find in Europe and once were common here. The quality is invariably better, and the help know their products and are anxious to please.

Quality is a powerful Retro-theme, and one that ties in closely with what people are looking for in the 21st century. Quality used to be better in America, quality of products (think of as late as the 1950s) and quality of service (remember who ran traditional hardware stores, who knew everything they stock and gave sound, free advice on the best way to solve a hardware problem?). Quality offers the buyer something worth waiting for and having less often, which ties in with the growing reaction against overspending and consumer excess. Quality gives buyers something worth keeping; good design and solid workmanship never go out of style. A quality product will last, which saves the buyer money over time; one Retro-person is still using the water-trap Rexair vacuum cleaner his grandmother bought in 1938, an expensive product then and now, but one that has easily paid for itself many times over in almost eighty years of service. In most things, Retro equals quality, and that is one of the reasons Retroculture is fast gaining ground.

Just as Retro-people like to buy quality products, so they also like to spend their quality time with other Retro-people. The need for suitable gathering places for Retro people offers another business opportunity. Several revivals of old-fashioned gathering places have already occurred, including amusement parks. Places like King's Dominion, Virginia, aren't really much different from such famous old amusement parks as Cedar Point, Ohio. They offer wholesome family entertainment, just as their predecessors did; the main difference may be that you took the trolley to the old amusement parks (many were actually built by the trolley lines as a way to increase ridership), and now you drive. Maybe some enterprising Retro-entrepreneur will reverse the historic process and build a trolley line to reach the amusement park!

There are many other business opportunities still to be explored in offering Retro gathering places. For starters, how about bars and nightclubs without blasting, electronically amplified music that is so loud it makes conversation impossible? A revival of the jazz club of the 1930s and 40s, with purely acoustic music (which sounds better anyway), might attract quite a following. Bars could reflect different as — perhaps the turn of the century or the Prohibition era, the time of the "speakeasy." The London 1940s nightclubs mentioned in the first chapter offer a model; they have become central elements in the lives of London's Retro crowd.

The 1930s dance hall offers another business opportunity. A few of the originals, like Cleveland's Avalon, still survive and do a good business. Many Retro people would love to spend Friday or Saturday night dancing the old dances to real big-band music. By offering music and dancing from the past, without screaming amplifiers or wild rock bands, old-fashioned dance halls would offer a safe, respectable place for people to gather — something that has grown hard to find in many cities.

In fact, the whole area of entertainment offers tremendous Retro-business opportunities. More and more Americans are tired of entertainment that is violent or suggestive, and they yearn for the kind of safe and decent entertainment our grandparents enjoyed. For example, imagine a revival on network television of the 1950s series, *I Remember Mama*. Set in the 1890s, that series portrayed a good solid Victorian family confronting and overcoming life's many challenges through sound values. Think how many American families today could relate to a series like that, because that is the kind of family they still want to be. Retro-themes like admiration for the Victorians might offer network television what it needs to reverse its decline in audience share.

As we noted in an earlier chapter, a good deal is already happening in the area of Retro-entertainment. But many new business opportunities are waiting to be explored, from "Retro Radio" (stations that re-create what you might have heard had you turned on the radio in an earlier era) through the revival of Chautaquas.[18] Virtually everything

---

18 "Chautauqua" was the term for an adult education movement popular in North America between the late-19th and early-20th centuries, noted for their mixture of entertainment, culture and education through live speakers, musicians etc. — Editor.

people used to enjoy is subject to revival, which gives Retro-people far more entertaining things to choose from than modern people can enjoy.

In each of the areas we have touched on here, we have only ventured to offer a few examples of possible Retro-business opportunities, as illustrations. Any new wave of fashion offers business opportunities. But Retroculture offers far more than most, because it includes more aspects of people's lives, it appeals to a wide diversity of eras, each with its own fashions, and it promises to be lasting. Enough Americans have come to realize that the past was better than what we have now that a grand effort to recapture the best things from the past will become our national course. It will be the theme that guides our country into the 21st century. Those who are first to help others grasp the theme may rightly expect to profit from their good works.

FIGURE 8. Yale Hardware Store, Cannon Falls, Minnesota. Now the Family Salon. (Source: McGhiever, Wikimedia Commons)

CHAPTER XI

∽

Retro-Service

ECONOMISTS TALK A LOT THESE DAYS about how we are becoming a "service economy." Most ordinary people find themselves asking, "If that's true, where is the service?" It sure seems hard to find. No matter whom we deal with — plumbers, contractors, waiters, clerks in stores, auto salesmen, you name it — we just can't seem to get the reliable, knowledgeable, polite and honest service we can remember from times past. And that's a shame, because real service doesn't cost any more to give, but it makes the world a much nicer place for everybody. Further, just as we all look for service on occasion, so we all also offer it at some point. Either way, we can make our lives and the lives of others better by getting it right — by reviving what the word "service" used to mean.

The starting point is to realize something our ancestors knew well: service is honorable. In fact, all human achievement is built on service, on doing something for someone else. That's how children get reared and taught, new products are invented and built and marketed, towns are founded and developed, religion is preached and spread — all through service. Service may be to family, friends, neighbors, customers, employers, the public, God — at root, it's all the same thing, doing something for someone else. Even Christ came, as He said, "to serve, not to be served."

Good service requires putting other people first and controlling self-gratification. That may explain why it has gotten so hard to find. Since the mid-1960s, we have been told to put ourselves first. From "Do your own thing" and "If it feels good, do it" through "You are what you own" and "Whoever dies with the most toys wins," recent times have celebrated self-centeredness. The results are all too evident in workers who don't do a good job, managers who pay themselves huge salaries and bonuses while their company goes bankrupt, and politicians whose greed knows no bounds.

It didn't used to be that way. Our forefathers believed self-centeredness was a vice. They knew real happiness came from serving others, not from trying to satisfy the endless demands of a rapacious self. That's why they found their lives growing richer with real achievement and satisfaction as they grew older, while ours become emptier. We have built on sand: they built on rock, the rock of good service honorably rendered.

You may be able to remember some of the ways in which good service and the people who gave it were honored. Think of how folks used to look up to missionaries (as some still do), those men and women who have left all the comforts of home to go and bring religion to the poor and friendless in far corners of the earth. They are people who know how to serve! Perhaps your grandparents' and great-grandparents' families had servants (many people back then did). If so, you may have heard stories about how those old family "retainers" were treated as members of the family and cared for in their later years. That was regarded as honor they had earned with their years of service. Perhaps one of your ancestors was a small-town doctor or storekeeper, a person highly respected for the service he gave his community. Regardless of how people served, service was respected, honored, and regarded as a good thing.

Retroculture seeks to brings good service back, to make it honorable once more — much more honorable than the selfishness that has replaced it. It means practicing many of the virtues children used to learn in school in all our dealings with other people. It means being attentive and helpful to others — to all others, not just the rich or the young and handsome. In fact, the person who values service will be especially helpful to the elderly or infirm, the handicapped, children, and others who may have no way to return anything but their thanks.

Good service means respect — respect both ways, whether you are the person serving or the one being served. (Mutually helpful formality, like use of last names with Mr., Mrs., or Miss, instead of first names is a good example of helpful formality.)

It means punctuality, which is really "being there" for others. In the old days, this was sometimes called "the courtesy of kings," because monarchs knew others had to wait for them no matter how late they were. Good kings and queens weren't late.

Good service means old-fashioned diligence: working hard. Nowadays, some people think they're being clever if they loaf on the job as much as possible, only working when someone might be watching. Ever go in a store and find all the clerks staring at their smartphones and carefully ignoring you, the customer? They are giving bad service both to you and to the store owner, the person who pays their salary. In the old days, loafers were looked upon with contempt; in contrast, hard work was praised and honored. Retroculture again honors diligence as a virtue, because it is essential to good service.

There is one final thing good service requires, and that is honesty. From sad experience, many Americans have two words come to mind when they want to define bad service: "car salesman." Why? Because too often, they've had car salesmen lie to them. The salesman swore the car was solid and dependable, and instead it proved a lemon. In contrast, a good service person is honest. If the special in the restaurant that night isn't very tasty, the good waitress warns her customers away from it. If the doohickey in the hardware store doesn't perform as claimed, the good clerk tells his customers. And the good car salesman (there are some) steers potential customers away from models he knows have serious defects. Without honesty, good service simply isn't possible — nor is anything else good.

RETRO-SERVICE IS GOOD BUSINESS

In a time when the real economy just sputters along and good jobs are hard to find, many people are concerned about the company they work for. They want it to do well, because if it goes under, they may be facing unemployment. Well, good service, Retro-service, is good business. It offers products the customers want, it makes those products to a high standard, it delivers them in ways the customers find both efficient and pleasant, and it makes customers want to come back. Think of how your grandparents often patronized the same businesses for decades, maybe even all their lives. They did so because those establishments gave them good old-fashioned service, service that often went beyond what most people today would expect or even imagine. In 1949, Mr. William A. Sturgiss bought a new Ford from the agency in Grantsville, Maryland where he had always bought his cars. He had bought two-door models in the past, but this time he decided to get a four-door. A few weeks after he took delivery of the car, the owner of the dealership called to ask how he liked it. Mr. Sturgiss said it ran fine, but he wished he had stuck with the two-door model. "I can take care of that," said the dealer. "Just bring it back and we'll give you a two-door instead." Which he did — at no charge. That's the kind of service that keeps a customer for life.

OFFERING RETRO-SERVICE

Retro-service usually doesn't cost any more to offer than typical modern slipshod service. Mostly it is a matter of politeness, knowledge, and a genuine desire to be helpful. It begins with good manners: calling customers "sir" or ma'am," or using their last names with Mr., Mrs., or Miss in front of it. Then, it requires really knowing the product or service you are offering. American automobile companies have had to learn the hard way about how important knowledgeable salesmen are to potential customers. For years, while foreign car companies stressed technical information about their cars in their ads and in their salesmens' pitches, Detroit ran ads with pretty girls sitting on the hoods of their cars and had their salesmen talk price. In effect, they talked down to car buyers, and the buyers went elsewhere, to someone who talked facts. The same is true for every business: the salesman who really knows the product shows he takes the customer seriously. From the customers' standpoint, that is an essential part of good service. It also used to be a maxim for salesmen: a good salesman knows his product. Like most of the old maxims, it's still true.

The past can suggest many specific ideas for offering good service. You may want to do some research into the history of whatever field you work in, to see how companies similar to yours offered good service. For example, home delivery used to be common for many businesses. Not only did homes have the services of the milkman, the bread man, and the egg lady, many grocery stores also delivered. Some are starting to do so again.

Another way some businesses used to offer good service was by putting their people in uniform. Recently, a new owner of a gas station in New England put all his people in uniforms, old-fashioned uniforms like gas station attendants used to wear, bow ties and all. His business soared, because to his customers the uniforms carried a message of good service. Similarly, an old bank in New England has no tellers with windows. It has never had them: it simply never changed from the days in the early 19th century when you sat down at a desk with a banker when you went to a bank, the way rich clients of big banks still do. In effect, every customer at this small bank gets his own "investment banker" — and the bank does very well, because people like its Retro service.

In service as in other matters, the past is an endless treasure chest we may draw on for ideas about how to do things better. Just as Retro-people study the past to find better ways to design and furnish their houses, entertain themselves, travel and even dine, so you may turn to history to discover ways to improve the service you and your business can offer.

Your reward will be happier customers, who return their loyalty as thanks for your service. And that means better business for you.

SERVING THE "PUBLIC GOOD"

The "public good" is one of those nice Victorian notions Retroculture makes fashionable again. Victorians believed not only in self-improvement, but also in improving the community in which they lived. They devoted substantial time and energy to public service: to helping the poor, teaching Sunday schools, fighting drunkenness through the Temperance League, working against "machine politics" in the Good Government movement, and many other similar efforts. They believed that every citizen owed service to his country and his community—to the "public good."

Retroculture seeks to revive this kind of good service just as it does good service in business. Our modern communities have as much or more need for service-minded volunteers as did communities in the 19th century. Crime, broken homes, poverty and the drug problem cannot be solved just through government programs. They need people, people who believe in service and want to offer their service to making their community a better place to live.

Many Americans already offer service to their communities in a wide variety of ways. At home, they recycle and compost to keep the town's landfill from overflowing. On their street, they participate in the local Block Watch and offer a helping hand to their neighbors.

They volunteer at the local library or hospital. They serve in the soup kitchen run by their church. They volunteer their time with the Red Cross and support it with donations. They canvass their neighborhood for one charity or another. All these are examples of service to the public good.

By looking back toward the past for guidance, Retroculture can add several dimensions to this ongoing effort at volunteer service. For one thing, it can tell us how important and effective such volunteer activities can be. Mid and late 19th-century America faced some serious social problems, many of which were solved or at least reduced through the efforts of volunteers. Drunkenness was a widespread public evil, a destroyer of many a working-class family and a blight on countless communities. Volunteers, working through churches, in politics, and through groups like the Womens' Christian Temperance Union, greatly reduced the excessive use of alcohol. They educated people as to its dangers, got through laws controlling the sale of alcohol, convinced people to take the "Temperance Pledge" not to drink, and through groups like Alcoholics Anonymous offered people a source of treatment for alcoholism.

Similarly, volunteers established a wide network of homes for single young women who had become pregnant, offering them places to live while they had their child and support in building a new life with their baby or finding a family who would adopt it. That network brought about a substantial reduction in the incidence of abortion. These examples from the past tell us that service really is important — it makes a measurable difference in society.

The past can also give us some lessons in how to be effective in serving the public good. It warns us against going too far — as the effort to curb alcohol did when it resulted in Prohibition. It also tells us that we can do more when we unite with other people working in the same cause. Many of today's best known public service organizations got started when an individual went beyond working alone and began to organize. Clara Barton, founder of the American Red Cross, is a good example.

Perhaps most important, the past tells us not to wait for someone else to do it: to identify a need, find or create a group or organization, and begin doing good work. As in so many other fields, the Victorians were men and women of action when it came to serving the public good. They took the initiative as individuals, locally and nationally, seeing what needed to be done and doing it. Now as then, that is called leadership, and it is essential to public service. Where some lead, others will follow, until, like the Victorians, we can see our society becoming a safer, healthier, better ordered place, for us and for our children.

If the Victorians could talk to us about serving the public good, they would say something people today might find surprising. They would tell us that though they were gratified by the public improvements their service made possible, that was not the most important thing they accomplished through it. The most important difference was the one it made in them.

In the past, service was not seen as being only something you did twice a week for a couple of hours on behalf on this or that organization. Rather, it was a way of life — a way of life opposite to the self-centeredness that has become fashionable in America. Serving was a check people used on their own thinking and behavior, a way of escaping self-centeredness and practicing another of those old-fashioned virtues, humility. 19th century Boston was shocked when one of its premier citizens, Mrs. Gardner (her home is now a splendid art museum), got down on her hands and knees to scrub the cathedral steps on Good Friday. But she was merely doing dramatically what many of our grandparents and great-grandparents did with less flair: curbing her own pride through service.

Often, this service was quiet, hardly even visible to others. It was service within the family, by taking care of the failing parents or alcoholic brother or retarded child, and doing it uncomplainingly and with love. Or, it was service in the church, as one of the unsung women who kept everything going by their long hours of service behind the scenes. Or it was service within the workplace, as the strong partner in the firm who kept it solvent in the face of laziness or incompetence on the part of others. "Covering for" other people who were too weak to carry their fair share of the load was a common way countless people served.

And by this service, however it was rendered, those who served were transformed. We may remember a favorite great aunt or grandparent who had undergone this transformation. Their "self," the demanding, I-want-mine part of human nature, had grown so thin the light came right through it. They had a happiness and peace so deep it was comforting just to be near them. None of life's little crises rattled them. They had grown beyond all stress. Their shoulders were broad enough to carry lightly whatever burdens others could not bear. And they got this way by serving, by putting others first in everything they did — by service as a way of life.

Self or service? That is one of the most important decisions every person makes. Which one will be first in your life? Modern fashion tell us to put self first. The past says otherwise, and so does Retroculture. Service, not self, is the basis of the life well lived, the race well run.

FIGURE 9. The Neiman-Marcus Headquarters and Flagship Store in Downtown Dallas. (Source: User 020808 at English Wikipedia)

CHAPTER XII

∽

Retro-America

EVER SINCE THE PILGRIMS LANDED at Plymouth, Massachusetts in 1620, Americans have looked confidently toward the future. They have expected life in the future to be better, for them, their children, and their children's children.

In recent years, we have lost this vision of a happier future. In the face of crime, family breakups, falling living standards and a host of other problems, Americans have become pessimistic. To more and more people, it seems as if our nation's great days lie in the past.

These concerns have two messages for us. The first is that people are not happy with the way things are or where they seem to be going. The second is that the past offers hope for the future. People want to recapture the good things from the past and bring them to life again. If we can do that, if the past can become the future, then the future can be bright — as bright and hopeful, safe and comforting as life in America used to be.

Retroculture's message is that we can do that. What we did once, we can do again. What worked once before will work again. And people know it.

Further, it is going to happen. In fact, it is already happening. All across America, people are rediscovering the past and working to bring it to life again. They are doing it on their own, in their own lives and the lives of their families and communities. They are doing it in millions of small steps. But put together, those millions of small steps add up to a great leap.

Just how far can Retroculture take us? What might a future Retro-America look like, an America where many people were consciously working to rediscover the good things from the past and bring them back to life? Let us allow our imagination to wander forward a bit, say about twenty years, to the year 2038, and see what we see…

The Saturday, January 23, 2038 real estate section of the *Cleveland Plain Dealer* includes an ad for homes in the new Retro-town of Alberta, east of Cleveland:

"Ride a Mile and Smile the While," on the fast new Light Rail line that connects Alberta with downtown Cleveland in less than forty minutes.

That's just one of the benefits of Retro-living in Alberta, northern Ohio's premier new-old town. Not a "development" but a real town, Alberta offers all the comforts of life a century ago. Victorian, Queen Anne and Craftsman homes line shady streets, all in easy walking distance of the car-free downtown. Stores, restaurants, and offices are just a stroll away, in a charming Victorian town center where families gather on the green for band concerts, softball games and just socializing. Churches and schools are part of the neighborhood too, and every house has a back yard big enough for a good size garden. Alberta also offers apartments and condominiums "up over the store" right downtown, and at modest prices.

The fast, quiet Light Rail line offers easy access to jobs in Cleveland and in nearby industrial parks. When the workday is over, it whisks you home to a place where life is as it used to be. Every house has a front porch, where people sit in the evening, talking with passers-by and watching the kids play safely in the street (Alberta's residential streets are also car-free from seven to nine o'clock every evening all through the summer). Noise controls mean you go to sleep every evening with the windows open, hearing nothing louder than the crickets singing. And Alberta's charter includes town-meeting government, so the people who live there, not outsiders, set the rules. Alberta is filling up fast, and it won't be expanded to where you'd need to drive to get around. If you are tired of junky highways, strip shopping centers, and developments where no one knows their neighbors, come take a look at Alberta and see what life in a real community is like. Just take the Red Line on the Rapid to Windermere and transfer to the Eastern Ohio Traction interurban. You'll soon understand why we named our town for Queen Victoria's beloved husband, Prince Albert. It's just the sort of place where Victorians will feel at home.

The March 3, 2038 issue of *Time* magazine's cover story is "The New Civility":

On the subway, no woman stands while a man sits. Gentlemen not only readily offer a seat, they hold packages, open doors, and tip their hats to ladies. Young people are careful not to make noise that would disturb others. When they speak to their elders, they say "Ma'am" or "Sir." No favor, however modest, does not receive a "thank you." On the road, a driver needing a "break" to get into traffic is promptly offered one, and cars stop for a pedestrian who merely approaches a crosswalk. Shoppers are careful to leave their cart so they don't block others coming down the aisle in the supermarket.

In a remarkable transformation, America has become a land of civility. Visitors from overseas, even from such traditionally polite places as Japan, are struck by the remarkably good manners they find here. It seems as if the whole nation is taking part in a good-natured contest to see who can be most polite. One British visitor commented, "In London, people just shove on by you. Here, they nod, smile, and apologize for being in your way when you are in theirs! They are wonderfully helpful to a poor visitor trying to find her way around. It is a bit embarrassing — we English are supposed to have good manners, but compared to you we're rude." In Tokyo, the Asahi Shimbun ran a series on "Learning from America"; the first article was on "Americans' Wonderful Manners."

It wasn't always like this. Twenty years ago, it seemed that people often went out of their way to be rude to others. Cars drove around with radios blaring. People went downtown or got on trains and airplanes dressed in little more than their underwear. Kids prided themselves on their threatening looks and mumbled monosyllabic answers to adults' inquires. Aggressiveness, selfishness, and thoughtless if not calculated rudeness seemed to govern relations with strangers and even with customers, neighbors and friends.

Fortunately, some Americans remembered or learned about a more distant past, those golden years in the late 19th and early 20th centuries when ladies were honored, gentlemen were respectful and children were discreet. By the 2020s, these Retro-Americans were showing the rest of us how life should be lived. It didn't have to be nasty, brutish and short; it could be quite agreeable, if only people would follow some simple, common-sense rules. Most of the rules boiled down to the Golden Rule: Do unto others as you would have them do unto you.

So good manners became fashionable again, and civility is now the hottest style. If you're a boor and want a date, a job or anyone's respect, forget it. Not that there's any excuse now for not knowing how to show good manners, since they are taught in schools, practiced on the job and around the family dinner table, and shown in every television show, even the soap operas. The new civility has made its mark on a new century, and it doesn't seem likely to fade with time. It's just too nice to let go.

Amtrak's annual report for the year 2037 reveals a new world of comfortable, relaxing Retro-travel: Last year, for the first time since World War II, most American travel was by train. Amtrak's 22,364 daily intercity and commuter trains accounted for 50.7% of all miles traveled in the United States by all modes of passenger transport.

More important to Amtrak was the reason most Americans now chose to travel by train. Extensive surveys of Amtrak's passengers revealed that 72.8% travelled by train because they preferred it over any other mode. In other words, almost three quarters of Amtrak's customers could have traveled by car or airplane, but chose the train because it offered the most enjoyable journey.

Amtrak's management attributes this remarkable revival of train travel primarily to its decision, taken in 2022, to model its future trains on those of the "Great Days of Rail Travel," the period from 1900–1930. Beginning that year, Amtrak ordered new passenger equipment that duplicated the cars from a century ago. Of course, this new equipment incorporated technical refinements that enhanced passenger comfort, such as air conditioning. But Amtrak's "Retrofleet" offered the feeling of the great trains: high clerestory ceilings with art glass windows, wood-paneled interiors with plush seats, elegant dining cars with linen table cloths, fine china, heavy silver and memorable food, and open-platform observation parlor cars where:

> Phoebe Snow could take the air
> Without a care
> While she did go
> Along the Road to Buffalo.

In 2025, Amtrak launched the first of its new Retrofleet in the now world-famous New York to San Francisco transcontinental expresses, the eastbound *Capitalist* and westbound *Manifest Destiny*. These all-Pullman, extra-fare trains, which offer every aspect of luxury Edwardian travel, were immediate hits with the traveling public and significant revenue successes for Amtrak. Today each train runs in at least five sections daily and both are sold out months in advance.

The success of the *Capitalist* and the *Manifest Destiny* was duplicated on virtually every route that Amtrak re-equipped with Retrofleet coaches, sleepers and diners. Public response was overwhelming. Huge crowds attended the exhibits of the new equipment held in major cities and welcomed the first re-equipped trains through their towns. Politicians lined up to promote the route through their state to be next to get the new cars.

Most important, people rode the new trains. They rode once to satisfy their curiosity, but having tasted real travel, travel as it used to be, they kept coming back. Speed had little to do with it; while average train speed was increased some, Amtrak offers true high-speed rail service (over 150 miles per hour) only in a few corridors. Service was definitely a factor. Amtrak was careful to make sure its employees offered respectful, dependable, efficient Retro-service to go along with its Retrofleet of cars. Increased train frequency, which offered more convenient travel, and careful tie-in of Amtrak trains with the new trolley systems many cities have built were both contributors.

But we would be less than honest if we did not admit that much of the success of Amtrak's new Retro-trains is due to a change in how Americans live their lives. People today are less in a hurry to get somewhere and more interested in enjoying the journey of life itself. We see it in everything: in the restoration of community in our towns and cities, in the volunteer efforts that have greatly lessened many of our social problems, in the general reorientation of life from having things to doing things. Inspired and guided by a great national rediscovery of our past and determination of recover what was best in it, Americans from every walk of life have remade the way we live.

Amtrak is proud to offer its Retro-trains as our contribution to this new-old America. It is a good place to live. And, relaxing over a fine dinner in the dining car while the best show in the world, America itself, rolls by the windows, it is also a good place to travel.

The annual Christmas catalogue of Dallas's Neiman-Marcus department store, with its wildly luxurious and imaginative special presents, has long been an American fixture. In the year 2038, those special presents include:

CHAPTER XII. RETRO-AMERICA

- **The "Upstairs, Downstairs" townhouse.** An exact reproduction, inside and out, of the Bellamy's townhouse as seen in the recently revived television classic, "Upstairs, Downstairs," is the perfect setting for Edwardian living. Built in the community and setting of your choice, it is the ideal wedding gift or retirement present for those who "have everything." Fully staffed including an English butler who answers to the name of "Hudson," it offers all you need to travel back in time, including closets already brimming with the latest turn-of-the-20th-century clothes in your sizes. It comes with either a coach-and-four or a motor car from the early 1900s, your choice. Price $7,500,000 plus property.

- **Your own Zeppelin airship.** For the man whose friends all have private airplanes and who wants to stand out in the crowd, we offer this year a genuine Zeppelin, built in Friedrichshafen, Germany. This 8,000,000 cubic foot airship, 840 feet long, can accommodate fifty people in absolute comfort, cruises at 90 miles per hour, and offers a unique view of the world through the glass floor of its smoking lounge (just like the *Hindenburg*). Comes equipped with aluminum grand piano, captain and trained crew. It's filled, of course, with non-flammable helium. Be the first to offer your family and guests air travel in the grand manner! Price $65,000,000. Hanger extra.

- **A Victorian aunt.** You and your family want to live as people did when Queen Victoria reigned, but you're not quite sure how to go about it. The solution? Your own Victorian aunt, to serve as your preceptor, guide, and leader through the wonderful Victorian years! A docent, fully educated in all the subtleties of Victorian manners, morals, styles and entertainments from giving a grand formal dinner to raising the children right, will reside with you for a full year and serve as your "Aunt Agatha." Leading by her own good and upright example, as aunts once did, she will gently draw your family back into the happy ways of Victorian times. Give your children the upbringing you wish you'd had, and give yourself the well-ordered Victorian home money just couldn't buy—until now! Price $350,000.

- **A private turn-of-the-century trolley car, just for you!** Many cities—including Dallas—now have "light rail systems," which is the new name for a streetcar line. Streetcars are a great way to get around any town. They are quiet, smooth riding, and non-polluting. But like any public conveyance, streetcars have their drawbacks, such as schedules you may not always find convenient and the presence of people to whom you have not been introduced. This year, Neiman Marcus offers the ideal way to enjoy your city's light rail system with the comfort and privacy you've come to expect—your own private streetcar! Built in Portugal to a turn-of-the-last-century American design, the Neiman Marcus trolley car offers a rich mahogany with inlaid rosewood interior, plush leather couches and richly upholstered armchairs, a small kitchen and serving area, and even a bathroom. Two 125-h.p. motors offer brisk acceleration and a top speed of fifty-five miles per hour, while twin trolley poles and controls at each end offer the convenience of bi-directional operation without a turntable. Hire a crew from your local transit authority or learn to operate the car yourself! Price $750,000, plus lead-in track from your home to the nearest trolley line. Carbarn available for $175,000 extra. Requires 600 volt DC power.

- **An 18th-century weekend.** Belle Grove plantation, in the Blue Ridge mountains of Virginia, is yours for a weekend of 18th-century living. You will dine on 18th-century dishes authentically prepared before an open fire, entertain your family and friends with a fox hunt and an 18th-century ball, sleep in a four-poster bed with corn husk mattress and supervise "your" house servants and field hands. You've read about how our Colonial forebears lived — now you can experience it yourself, right down to "close stools" and a sedan chair. Your plantation's overseer, an expert on all aspects of 18th-century life, will guide you through a weekend you will always remember. Price $8,500 for a family of four. One-week stay $24,500.

The CBS Evening News for May 17, 2038, included this report:

> The White House tonight hosts the first public performance of the winners in what President Miller has announced will be an annual event, the Presidential Contest in Retro-music Composition. Earlier today, we met with the President in the Oval Office to get a hint about what the nation will be hearing tonight.
>
> Interviewer: Mr. President, you have sought during your term in office to make the White House a center of our national cultural rival. How does this new contest fit into that?
>
> President Miller: Personally, I think music — good music — is one of the most important products of any nation. We all know how low music had sunk in the last decades of the 20th century and the first part of the 21st. Most of it was just noise, played at deafening volume. It was 'anti-music,' if you will. By starting this contest and playing the winning compositions here at the White House for their premier we are marking the new era in music this century has brought. Teddy Roosevelt said the Presidency was a 'bully pulpit.' I want to make it a 'bully conductor's podium' as well, to give the good 'new old' music that is now being written the public attention and honor that it merits.
>
> Interviewer: Can you give us any hints about what we will be hearing tonight?
>
> President Miller: As you know, the contest was for symphonic compositions, written in one of three styles: Baroque, Classic, or Romantic. We had a number of splendid entries in each category, and I am sure you will be hearing many of them, not just the winners, performed by orchestras around the country. I might give a hint by saying the romantic winner

reminds me of Brahms, the classic winner of Haydn, and the very unusual baroque winner of Biber. I confess the baroque piece is my own favorite.

Interviewer: What led to this 'Retro-music,' to writing new music in old styles?

President Miller: By the end of the last century, it was obvious music had taken a 'wrong turn' somewhere along the line. Just where is a matter of dispute, but there was no disputing the fact itself.

As early as the 1990s, a few signs appeared pointing not forwards, but backwards — back to musical styles that had held up over time, Baroque, Classic, Romantic. The opera *The Ghosts of Versailles*, premiered in 1992, is an example. While most of its music was modern, it contained a number of pieces written in an 18th-century style — Retro-music. Just as classic style had returned in architecture first through decorative bits attached to International-style glass boxes, then caught on and became general for whole buildings, so Retro-music bits and pieces began turning up in other compositions and repertoires. People loved it and demanded more of it.

The real breakthrough, as you probably know, was Richard Cher's *Homage a la Classique* symphony in 2024. Its premier at Carnegie Hall entranced the house. It was not just that Cher wrote in the Classic style, the style of Mozart and Haydn, that reigned from about 1760 to around 1800. Cher's achievement was to write one of the best symphonies of that style ever heard. The audience at the premier knew within a few dozen measures that they were hearing history being made, that this composition would move and thrill audiences for centuries, the same way the overture to Mozart's *Don Giovanni* moved and thrilled them. Cher had equaled Mozart. That was a stunning achievement.

The point was not lost on other composers: it was possible to write extraordinary new music in old styles. Those styles were in no sense played out. And thus, the Retro-music movement was born. Tonight, we will hear how far it has come.

Interviewer: But why hold this premier of what is, after all, only music, here at the White House? Why should a President of the United States be involved with music?

President Miller: Only music? I think you, and the American people, know better than that. Is a nation nothing but figures in a ledger book, so much money taken in, so much given out for this or that purpose? I don't think so. A nation has a soul, and that soul is defined in its culture. If the soul is ignored or degraded, as ours was in the late-20th and early 21st century, the nation decays and eventually dies. The great turnaround in America's course in this century came not from economics or politics, but from our cultural recovery — from the return of beauty to art and architecture, from the recovery of a sense of community in our towns and cities, from the rediscovery of family, home, and civic duty.

When I was a young man, I saw a cartoon in *The New Yorker* I never forgot. It showed a couple of angels welcoming an arriving soul into Heaven. One of the angels said, 'Oh goody! You're just in time for Mozart's symphony in G.K. 33,678.' I thought then, if Heaven means hearing new Mozart symphonies through all eternity, how might we bring a bit of Heaven down to earth?

Tonight, the American people will hear an answer to that question. I can't think of a better way the White House could serve this country. Can you?

Interviewer: No, Mr. President, I can't.

An article in the October issue of *Travel and Leisure* recommends a visit to a Retro-community in Pennsylvania:

The growth of Retro-communities — new or restored towns where people live as they did in earlier times — has made travel in America a wondrous thing. You can visit frontier towns, quaint Victorian villages, 18th-century cities (see the article on New Philadelphia in our June issue), even Harlem in Manhattan, now restored to its 1920s greatness.

In the beautiful country of Pennsylvania's Laurel Highlands, you can find still more: an entire rural county that has chosen to go back in time, to the early years of the 20th century. Pennultima, as the "settlement" is known to those who live there, is akin to the Shaker colonies of the 19th century. It is much more than restored buildings and ice-cream socials in the town square on summer Saturday evenings (though the county seat, Somerset, has those too). It is a determined effort by a band of visionary people to recapture life as it was more than a century ago.

Pennultima began almost twenty years ago, in the city of Pittsburgh. There, a Retro-club of people who were interested in turn-of-the-century America decided they wanted to do more than study that era. They wanted to re-create it. With about 250 members scattered throughout the Pittsburgh area, they knew there was not much they could do there. But if they all moved to one small town, there would be enough of them to re-make that town in the image they wanted.

They chose the town of Meyersdale, in Somerset county, not too far from Pittsburgh. They had no desire to impose their ways on anyone else, so they started by approaching the people of Meyersdale and explaining what they wanted to do.

The local folk were receptive. Meyersdale was a dying town. For decades, the young people had been moving away, leaving only the old. Once important for its coal and its location on two railroads, Meyersdale had been bypassed by the highway era and the mines had played out. By the 1950s, decay had set in. The buildings were run down, Meyers Avenue, the town's "rich row" of turn-of-the-century homes, grown shabby. Amtrak's trains no longer stopped there. One of the railroads, the Western Maryland, was converted into a beautiful bike trail.

But the people of Meyersdale knew that in the early 1900s, their town had been full of hope, bustle and opportunity. It had a good hotel, the New Colonial, a number of local industries including a Victrola factory, and even its own trolley line, the Pennsylvania and Maryland. They looked back on those years as their best time, and they were willing to join the outsiders from Pittsburgh in trying to recapture the Meyersdale of 1910.

So, in 2019, the Pittsburgh folks moved in. Some moved into town and bought old houses and restored them. Others bought farms around the town. They brought their business with them from Pittsburgh, commuting electronically — making new technology serve old ways of living. Meyersdale stirred and began to come to life again. There were more children in the schools (they fixed up the old school downtown to the way it had been early in the century and put it back in use), church congregations grew, and, because the newcomers shopped in town, the downtown again became a good place to succeed in business.

As word about Pennultima spread among Retroculture people nationwide, others began migrating in. Learning from the large local Amish population, some became farmers using old-fashioned techniques. Others moved into neighboring towns like Garrett and Berlin and into the county seat of Somerset. Here as in Meyersdale, the local people welcomed them. That's one of the nice things about Retroculture: no one feels threatened by it. It means safe towns and good neighbors, old-fashioned schools where children really learn, and quiet well-tended streets.

As Retroculture spread over the county, the people, newcomers and old-timers, joined together to take everything they could back in time. Many of them no longer owned cars. Instead, the trolley line was restored and extended to link all the towns and hamlets, and local trains, passenger and freight, were brought back on the railroads. Farm families were never far from a town where they could catch a train or trolley car, and bicycles or horses and wagons or buggies did fine for getting into town. Local, often one-room schools kept children close to home.

If you want to visit Pennultima today, you too will need to go back in time just to get there. You will leave your car at the edge of the county, in a parking lot near the end of the trolley line (one is conveniently located at Exit 10, Somerset, on the Pennsylvania Turnpike). Or, come by train, as you probably would have in 1910; Amtrak now offers ten trains each day stopping in Meyersdale.

For the visitor, the most impressive thing about Pennultima is that it does not feel like a place for tourists. Of course, it isn't. It's not a show, like Williamsburg or Plimoth Plantation. It's there for the people who live there, and even in the height of summer, they far outnumber the tourists. You quickly feel that this is something real.

Pennultima residents welcome visitors, in part because they really want to share what they've discovered with you, and in part because like most Retroculture people, they just want to be nice (that's why they've gone back to a nicer time, after all). Many of them first came to Pennultima as visitors themselves, fell in love with it and came back to stay. There's still plenty of room for newcomers.

The trolley line will whisk you silently along through some of the east's prettiest country. Unspoiled by the roar of traffic or the sight of mobile homes or satellite dishes, you see America as it was: quietly prosperous, well-tended, harmonious and at peace. You may if you choose also use the local trains, which are pulled by steam engines whose wonderful chuffing echoes softly from the surrounding hills.

Travel & Leisure took the trolley to where it all began, the borough of Meyersdale, for a fall weekend. Somerset county is a major maple sugar producer (Meyersdale hosts a Sugar Festival in the early spring, with special trains from Pittsburgh and Washington), and in the autumn the hills are radiant with the oranges and reds of the sugar maple leaves. We stayed in the New Colonial hotel, which has been refurbished beautifully to its as-new state and which also boasts an excellent dining room. The town has a number of small, mom-and-pop restaurants where you can find a breakfast of real buckwheat cakes, made with a sourdough starter, at very modest prices. The local bakery sells perfect picnic lunches, packed in returnable wicker baskets; we took ours up to the cemetery, on a hill overlooking the town, for a lunch with an unbeatable view. Somehow, we had the feeling that earlier generations of Meyersdale folks were glad to welcome us there to see the town they had been so proud of.

Because there are no automobiles in Somerset county, the roads are perfect for walking or bicycling (you can rent bicycles in every town). Or, do as we did Saturday afternoon and rent a buggy and team from the livery stable. The horses are docile and accustomed to inexpert hands, and the stable offers a short driving lesson to those new to the reigns. We drove out old route 219 towards Boynton, up and over Hunsrick mountain; the view is one of the best in the county, and no one will be behind you beeping a horn if you stop a while to gaze.

Our children, ages ten to twelve, had made friends Friday evening with a few of the local children, and we had no hesitation leaving them to play while we went for our drive. That's the kind of place Pennultima is. The wife of the minister of the Methodist church, which is just across and up the street from the hotel, said she'd keep an eye on them, and we knew she would.

Speaking of church, Meyersdale is full of churches, built in the late 19th and early 20th centuries in the town's first boom. You'll miss some of what Pennultima offers if you don't go on Sunday morning, when the whole town rings with bells. The people are welcoming, the choirs are large and good, and you quickly see that these people live what they believe in. We joined the Methodists that Sunday, in a church with a stunning barrel-vaulted ceiling and a fine pipe organ. As you would expect, the service book was that used at the beginning of the 20th century, with the fine old language the modern books have deleted. Somehow, it felt like church should. We were invited to join the coffee hour afterward, and discovered that Meyersdale women are enthusiastic bakers, with a strong influence from the local Amish and Mennonites. The *Apfelstrudel* was a gem, and the oatmeal cake with German icing, a local specialty, made for two very happy children.

Sunday afternoon we took off around the county by trolley to Rockwood enjoying the splendid fall colors, then by steam train back to Somerset, where we had left our car. The Summit diner, near the car parking lot and the turnpike, offered a halfway point between 1910 and today; it's a classic diner from 1960, with good, home-cooked American food.

We will not soon forget Pennultima, nor the people we met there. They were remarkably happy people. They had seen the past, and it worked. It was, and in Somerset country is, a time of children playing safely in the street, families all dressed up parading to church, fresh farm produce in little corner stores, the wonderful restful quiet that comes when machines are few, laundry flapping on backyard lines and horses clopping on brick streets, singing trolley wires and the aroma of fresh-baked cinnamon rolls drifting from a farmhouse kitchen. Walking in the evening up Meyers Avenue on the slate sidewalks and under the new-old streetlamps with their corrugated metal shades, listening to the quiet, looking in the windows at the beautifully restored Victorian and Edwardian interiors of the homes, heading to the B&O station to watch the westbound *Capitol Limited* come through, we had an overwhelming sense of what America had been, had lost, and here has regained.

As travelers, we have been to many places and seen many things. Most we have been happy to pass quickly by. Some have amused us for a while. A few we would return to. But only here, in Retro-America, would we happily have stayed.

Verweile doch! Du bist so schön...

OTHER BOOKS PUBLISHED BY ARKTOS

Sri Dharma Pravartaka Acharya	The Dharma Manifesto
Joakim Andersen	Rising from the Ruins: The Right of the 21st Century
Winston C. Banks	Excessive Immigration
Alain de Benoist	Beyond Human Rights
	Carl Schmitt Today
	The Indo-Europeans
	Manifesto for a European Renaissance
	On the Brink of the Abyss
	The Problem of Democracy
	Runes and the Origins of Writing
	View from the Right (vol. 1–3)
Arthur Moeller van den Bruck	Germany's Third Empire
Matt Battaglioli	The Consequences of Equality
Kerry Bolton	Revolution from Above
	Yockey: A Fascist Odyssey
Isac Boman	Money Power
Ricardo Duchesne	Faustian Man in a Multicultural Age
Alexander Dugin	Ethnos and Society
	Eurasian Mission
	The Fourth Political Theory
	Last War of the World-Island
	Putin vs Putin
	The Rise of the Fourth Political Theory
Edward Dutton	Race Differences in Ethnocentrism
Mark Dyal	Hated and Proud
Koenraad Elst	Return of the Swastika
Julius Evola	The Bow and the Club
	Fascism Viewed from the Right
	A Handbook for Right-Wing Youth
	Metaphysics of War

OTHER BOOKS PUBLISHED BY ARKTOS

	The Myth of the Blood
	Notes on the Third Reich
	The Path of Cinnabar
	Recognitions
	A Traditionalist Confronts Fascism
Guillaume Faye	*Archeofuturism*
	Archeofuturism 2.0
	The Colonisation of Europe
	Convergence of Catastrophes
	A Global Coup
	Sex and Deviance
	Understanding Islam
	Why We Fight
Daniel S. Forrest	*Suprahumanism*
Andrew Fraser	*Dissident Dispatches*
	The WASP Question
Génération Identitaire	*We are Generation Identity*
Paul Gottfried	*War and Democracy*
Porus Homi Havewala	*The Saga of the Aryan Race*
Lars Holger Holm	*Hiding in Broad Daylight*
	Homo Maximus
	Incidents of Travel in Latin America
	The Owls of Afrasiab
Richard Houck	*Liberalism Unmasked*
A. J. Illingworth	*Political Justice*
Alexander Jacob	*De Naturae Natura*
Jason Reza Jorjani	*Prometheus and Atlas*
	World State of Emergency
Roderick Kaine	*Smart and SeXy*
Peter King	*Here and Now*

OTHER BOOKS PUBLISHED BY ARKTOS

	Keeping Things Close
	On Modern Manners
Ludwig Klages	*The Biocentric Worldview*
	Cosmogonic Reflections
Pierre Krebs	*Fighting for the Essence*
Stephen Pax Leonard	*The Ideology of Failure*
	Travels in Cultural Nihilism
Pentti Linkola	*Can Life Prevail?*
H. P. Lovecraft	*The Conservative*
Norman Lowell	*Imperium Europa*
Charles Maurras	*The Future of the Intelligentsia & For a French Awakening*
Michael O'Meara	*Guillaume Faye and the Battle of Europe*
	New Culture, New Right
Brian Anse Patrick	*The NRA and the Media*
	Rise of the Anti-Media
	The Ten Commandments of Propaganda
	Zombology
Tito Perdue	*The Bent Pyramid*
	Morning Crafts
	Philip
	William's House (vol. 1–4)
Raido	*A Handbook of Traditional Living*
Steven J. Rosen	*The Agni and the Ecstasy*
	The Jedi in the Lotus
Richard Rudgley	*Barbarians*
	Essential Substances
	Wildest Dreams

OTHER BOOKS PUBLISHED BY ARKTOS

Ernst von Salomon	*It Cannot Be Stormed*
	The Outlaws
Sri Sri Ravi Shankar	*Celebrating Silence*
	Know Your Child
	Management Mantras
	Patanjali Yoga Sutras
	Secrets of Relationships
George T. Shaw (ed.)	*A Fair Hearing*
Oswald Spengler	*Man and Technics*
Richard Storey	*The Uniqueness of Western Law*
Tomislav Sunic	*Against Democracy and Equality*
	Homo Americanus
	Postmortem Report
	Titans are in Town
Hans-Jürgen Syberberg	*On the Fortunes and Misfortunes of Art in Post-War Germany*
Abir Taha	*Defining Terrorism*
	The Epic of Arya (2nd ed.)
	Nietzsche's Coming God, or the Redemption of the Divine
	Verses of Light
Bal Gangadhar Tilak	*The Arctic Home in the Vedas*
Dominique Venner	*For a Positive Critique*
	The Shock of History
Markus Willinger	*A Europe of Nations*
	Generation Identity
Alexander Wolfheze	*Alba Rosa*